TRAILS TO NATURE'S MYSTERIES
The Life of a Working Naturalist

TRAILS TO NATURE'S MYSTERIES
The Life of a Working Naturalist

ROSS E. HUTCHINS
Illustrated with photographs by the author

DODD, MEAD & COMPANY
New York

Frontispiece: *A trail in the Everglades*

1   2   3   4   5   6   7   8   9   10

Library of Congress Cataloging in Publication Data

Hutchins, Ross E
   Trails to nature's mysteries.

   Includes index.
   SUMMARY: The author describes his boyhood
in the Rocky Mountains, his developing interest in
plants and animals, and his experiences as a naturalist
in various parts of the United States and the world.
   1.   Hutchins, Ross E.—Juvenile literature.
2.   Naturalists—United States—Biography—Juvenile
literature.   [1.   Hutchins, Ross E.   2.   Naturalists]
I.   Title.
QH31.H86A34   500.9′2′4 [B] [92]   76–50554
ISBN 0–396–07401–4

To my wife, ANNIE LAURIE, in deepest appreciation of her aid and encouragement down the years. As a trained biologist, she deserves equal credit for whatever contributions I have made to the sum total of biological knowledge and understanding.

ACKNOWLEDGMENT

I WISH to give due credit to my sister, Lucille Bruce, for her aid in locating many pictures of our early years on the Montana cattle ranch. Her love of horses, even greater than my own, has endured the years. She and her husband now raise and show thoroughbred Arabians in the Land of Shining Mountains.

CONTENTS

FOREWORD

ON THIS COLD, rainy afternoon of an autumn day I sit before a roaring log fire deep in the Great Smoky Mountains. Conditions are perfect for thought and contemplation and, as is often the case, my thoughts drift back across the years to other times, mountains, and places, to the things I have seen and the things I have done during a career as a professional biologist and naturalist.

Almost since childhood I have been involved, one way or another, with the living world around me. First, there was the wonder of it all. Then, as knowledge replaced the wonder, I began delving into Nature's deeper mysteries, never completely satisfied by superficial observation, always looking for deeper meanings. It has been a long search for truth. Sometimes I found it, at other times it was as elusive as a summer rainbow. Along the way there has been satisfaction and, frequently, some amusing incidents.

In time, as a biologist turned writer-photographer, I sought to put into words and pictures the things I saw and felt. Thus, at last, I became a writer of popularized science, attempting to share my thoughts and experiences with others, which I assume to be a commendable endeavor.

This, then, is a species of autobiography in which, I hope, the reader may share my varied experiences, thrilling with me at the sight of a column of leaf-cutting ants streaming across the floor of a subtropical forest at midnight, of watching a mother alligator building her stick nest beside a Southern bayou, of watching at close range a cliff swallow applying her beakful of clay to a nest upon a cliff face high in the Rocky Mountains. Again, there have been amusing incidents in which I was an interested observer. I recall vividly a skunk battling an angry mob of yellowjackets beside a stream in the Great Smoky Mountains and of another skunk feeding contentedly while a pair of foxes watched avidly but very respectfully from a few yards away.

And so what follows are the experiences and small events in the life of a working naturalist. May you share with me the thrills of discovery and of firsthand observation of the strange and often amazing world of plant and animal life.

—Ross E. HUTCHINS

Elkmont, Tennessee

TRAILS TO NATURE'S MYSTERIES
The Life of a Working Naturalist

Cattle ranch in the high Rockies where I grew up. On either side rise pine-covered buttes and, beyond, the Madison Range. Some of the distant peaks reach 10,000 feet.

1
THE HIGH ROCKIES

I WAS bored with summer school. "School" was a makeshift classroom at our cattle ranch in the high Rockies of Montana. Also present in this converted bunkhouse were my sister Lucille and two children from a small ranch several miles up the Madison River. Half asleep, I gazed out the window, my eyes wandering away across the wide river toward the distant mountains. I could see my saddle horse down in the pasture and wished fervently that I were on his back. Suddenly I became aware of some large animal wading slowly across the river in our direction and it gradually dawned on me that it was a large bull moose.

I yelled at Miss Caldwell, our teacher, and pointed toward the river. Probably she had also been bored and welcomed a diversion. Anyway, she hurried out the door for a better view, followed by all of us. Outside, we realized that it was, indeed, a very large bull moose with great spreading antlers. School was out in an instant and we all rushed across the field below the ranch house for a better look. Wishing to be the first to see the animal close-up, I ran on ahead and did, indeed, obtain a much closer view than I had anticipated. Unknown to me, the moose had changed his course while hidden from view by a low hill and so, when I reached the crest of the hill, the moose and I met head-on. Suddenly the great beast stood before me less than ten feet away. He looked as large as a mountain, his great antlers spreading out from his head like trees. From his neck hung a "bell," or dewlap, nearly a yard long. We both stopped, the moose and I, regarding each other. I was frozen in my tracks and could not have moved if my life had depended on it.

For perhaps ten seconds the beast looked at me and stamped his feet. Time stood still. I was ten years old at the time but I can still feel my sudden fear, the abrupt contact with great and eminent danger. A bull moose, I had heard, can be very unpredictable. There had been several reports of people being attacked by them.

Fortunately, however, the incident came to an abrupt end when the moose turned and walked off, unhurried and regal, as befits such a great animal. In the meantime the others had joined me and we all watched as the moose disappeared into a grove of aspens along Cascade Creek. Unfortunately, Miss Caldwell suddenly remembered that school was supposed to be still in session and so herded us all back into the so-called schoolroom.

Not many people, I venture to say, have had their educations interrupted by a bull moose. There have been numerous other obstacles to learning, but rarely by such an incident. However, a year or so later something occurred at the Missouri Flat school on the other side of the Madison River that in some ways was even more serious.

This was a larger school with more pupils and a proper schoolhouse. About the middle of July a large bull buffalo appeared, from whence no one seemed to know. A buffalo, as many people know, can be very dangerous, so when this one turned up in the schoolyard the teacher was very much con-

cerned. There were about a dozen pupils, and the teacher attempted unsuccessfully to drive the buffalo away. Thus, there
developed a stalemate; the buffalo remained in the schoolyard
and the children and the teacher remained inside. This situation prevailed until dusk when some of the ranchers, concerned
over the whereabouts of their offspring, appeared on saddle
horses and drove the animal away. It disappeared into the
mountains and was never seen again.

The ranch where I spent my early years was, and is, located
in the Upper Madison Valley about forty miles above the small
cow town of Ennis. It was then wild country, very sparsely
settled. The Hutchins family controlled a segment of the wide
valley for a distance of six or eight miles, and the name, Hutchins Ranch, still appears on most Montana road maps.

Grandfather and his growing family had traveled west during the eighties by covered wagon, covering a large part of the
Northwest in search of gold. However, my grandmother, more
practical, had called a halt on the Madison River at the point
where West Fork joins it. This ranch had eventually become
the local center of life, social and otherwise, to the sourdoughs
still panning the creeks for gold and to the cowpunchers living
their lonely lives in cow camps back on the ranges. Frequently,
on Saturday nights, dances were held at the home ranch, at-
tended by people from considerable distances. One of these was
Spencer Watkins who spent the summer herding cattle on the
range about fifteen miles up the river. He would ride down to
the ranch, dance most all night, and be back with his cattle the
next day. The cattle he herded belonged to his family, which
had a large "spread" down near Ennis.

Many years later, Spencer Watkins visited me at the University where I eventually became a professor. He had changed
but little; he was still a cowpoke at heart, even though he had
just returned from a round-the-world cruise.

Mail came to the ranch once a week by stagecoach and was

© RAND MC NALLY & COMPANY, R.L. 76–Y–79

Portion of current road map showing the Hutchins Ranch (see circle at lower center).

sorted on the living room floor. The mail belonging to other people, mostly lone men living back in the mountains, was placed in a bank of pigeonholes on the wall. Now and then they appeared at the ranch for their mail and a free meal. Most of these were "characters" and I found them fascinating. There was West Fork Kelly who had mined gold all the way from Australia to the Klondike, settling down at last about ten miles up West Fork. There were also Missouri Bill and English Tom, the latter eventually inheriting the title of Earl as a member of the British peerage.

Such were the people I came to know as a young boy. Many a night I sat enthralled in the bunkhouse, listening to their tales of other years and far-off places. I decided that someday I would see some of the places they talked about.

Our own ranch was located a couple of miles above my grandfather's ranch and adjoined it. It was situated at a point where a beautiful little stream dropped down out of the Madison Range through a deep, forested canyon. This stream is known as Dead Man Creek, from an old story concerning two men who had once built a cabin and spent the winter there. When spring had come, according to the tale, only one man was seen. Presumably, he had killed the other one. Even though my parents and my sister and I lived up on Dead Man Creek, the old home ranch remained the actual center of my existence. My grandfather was something of a self-trained naturalist and probably had much to do with my early interests in natural history. Surrounding his living room walls were many glass cases holding what grandfather called his "curios." These included everything from a whale tooth to stuffed birds and mineral specimens. On rare occasions he could be badgered into unlocking some of the cases to let me actually handle some of his specimens. This was always a special treat.

Grandfather had a number of books, among which was one I especially liked. It was about Stanley's search for Livingstone

in Darkest Africa. I pored over the illustrations of strange
beasts and deep jungles. There were many pictures of white
men in colonial Africa, all of them wearing pith helmets or
topees. Apparently this was the standard headgear of that far
land and I vowed that someday I, too, would wear a pith
helmet and go exploring in tropical jungles. Years later I did
obtain and wear a pith helmet, but it was heavy and uncom-
fortable and I wondered why African colonials had worn them.
I still wonder.

Such things, no doubt, tended to center my interests in the
natural world around me. However, growing up alone in that
wild setting with few playmates, I was increasingly fascinated
by the local plants and animals. In spring I watched the birds
returning from southern climes and observed their nesting activities. In summer I rode or walked the mountain trails, catch-
ing brief glimpses of wild creatures. Winter brought me into

*The "home ranch," two miles down the Madison River and joining
our ranch. It was established by my grandfather in the 1880s.*

even closer contact with the birds that remained after the rest had gone south. Deer and elk, forced down from higher elevations by deep snows, congregated near the ranch, making it possible to observe them at close quarters. The deep snow was like a great slate upon which the wild animals left the records of their nocturnal activities. Often, while skiing in the mountains, I could reconstruct small happenings. Now and then I saw the tracks of mice in the snow and the wing marks of owls that had dropped down to capture them.

Realizing in what direction my interests were developing, my parents did much to encourage me. One Christmas they presented me with a copy of Anna Botsford Comstock's book, *Handbook of Nature-Study*. This, I quickly found, contained a gold mine of information about the plants and animals I saw. I studied the pictures and drawings and even tried to make my own drawings. Even though I never became an artist, in my mind was implanted the idea of somehow recording the things I saw. Later, this led to an interest in photography, the perfect medium for portraying wild things. Exactly how my early interests became centered on insects I am not sure. It is probable, however, that the acquisition of a book on the subject was responsible. This one was *Manual for the Study of Insects* by Professor John Henry Comstock, the husband of Anna Botsford Comstock. This well-worn book is still in my library and remains one of the best texts on the subject.

It was about this time that I acquired my own "laboratory." There was a small cabin located beside Dead Man Creek and here I was allowed to move my collections of butterflies and other insects, as well as my pressed plant specimens. I also moved my bed into this cabin from the upstairs room I had occupied in the ranch house.

From some source—where I do not recall—I had obtained a small electric generator. I toiled enthusiastically, building a small dam across the creek and then constructed a water wheel

This large boulder rolled down from the mountain during one of the frequent earthquakes. My "laboratory" is at the left.

having a pulley arrangement to drive the generator. I thus had a source of electricity. It was not very dependable but it did give me an electric light. Rural electricity was unheard of at that time and place.

By devious means I also acquired a fairly complete chemical outfit, enabling me to perform simple experiments. I realize now that some of my experiments were potentially dangerous and that I could easily have killed myself. For example, I decided one day to make some guncotton, which was supposed to be very explosive. According to a book I had, the process was simple; all I would have to do was to place some cotton in a mixture of nitric and sulphuric acids and then wash the cotton in water. This was supposed to nitrify the cotton, creating nitrocellulose or guncotton.

All went according to plan, and after the cotton had been well washed, I took it into the ranch house to dry. There I placed the cotton in my mother's warming oven. By then it was time for dinner and we all sat down to eat. Shortly, from the kitchen came a loud bang and I at once knew just what had happened; the guncotton had exploded. When I rushed into the kitchen a number of pots and pans lay on the floor, having been blown off the stove by the force of the explosion. I was strongly advised to confine my chemical experiments to my laboratory; if I wanted to blow that up it was my own business.

Such was my world, the only world I had known up to the age of about ten years. My formal schooling had been sketchy, consisting of a couple of summer terms at the ranch and some instruction by my mother. I could read and write and figured that was about all there was to education. However, my parents had other ideas. One fall morning my father informed me that I would be leaving the next day to enter school down at Ennis where I would stay with an aunt.

A short summer school was held at the ranch, using one of the bunkhouses as a schoolroom. The teacher lived at the ranch. Present were my sister Lucille (right) and I (left). The other two are from another ranch.

This, indeed, was bad news. I caught up my horse, old Snoozer, from the pasture and rode up the trail toward the mountains. During the previous night, the first snow of the season had fallen and the ground was white. Everywhere I could see the tracks and trails of wild creatures. Once I spotted the dark form of an elk, its great antlers etched against the sky. This had been my world and I could not imagine there being any other way of life. Going away to school seemed to signal the end of everything I had known and loved.

As I rode back down the trail toward the ranch house, I stopped my horse to gaze at the scene spreading away below. Perhaps, I thought, I can someday return, rich and famous. Old Snoozer would, of course, be gone. That would be sad. The future looked very bleak.

The morning of my departure arrived and I hid in my cabin, hoping that my parents would relent or forget about the whole thing. Unfortunately they had not forgotten; they came over to my cabin and called to me. I did not answer. When they came in they found me clinging to the bedpost like a leech, making it necessary for them to literally pry me loose by force.

Of the trip down to Ennis I have no recollections; I was numb with sorrow.

I was not happy in school; my entire way of life had not prepared me for confinement in a stuffy schoolroom. In the first place I was homesick. Anyone who has ever experienced this malady will agree that, especially to a child, it is a horrible feeling. Like seasickness, it may not be fatal but it may as well be.

Of my first weeks in school I have no fond memories. I presume that it was a good school, but I did not like it. I, at once, took up with the most unruly boys in the school. About a week after my enrollment it was rumored that the county nurse was due to arrive and "examine" us. My friends and I immediately decided that this was an ordeal we could not endure and so, after a short conference, we decided to "play hooky." We left the school and hurried down the hill and through the town's main and only street. On the way, at my two companions' suggestion, we stopped at Chowning's store and bought a plug of chewing tobacco.

The Madison River lies just beyond the town and when we arrived at this point we left the road and descended into the river bottom, entering a large grove of cottonwood trees. There we built a small fire and sat down to "enjoy" the chewing tobacco. Unfortunately I had never chewed tobacco before, but not to be outdone, I took a large chaw when my turn came—which turned out to be a grave error. To my surprise, the tobacco was hot and burning to my mouth. However, not wishing to admit this, I rushed away through the trees and washed out my mouth in the river. I have never tried chewing tobacco since. After getting rid of the tobacco I returned to the fire and sat down. Shortly it began to snow, a wet, fall snow that soon covered the ground and adhered to the leaves. I did not know how the others felt, but as for me, I wished that I was back at the warm school, nurse or no nurse.

The next morning the principal took all three of us into his office and lectured us, after which he applied a rubber hose where it would do the most good. I never "played hooky" again.

My parents came down to see me several times during the winter, the trips requiring about two days each way. The grades during the winter were drifted deeply, making it necessary to shovel through many of them. I had an uncle living at Cameron, about halfway between the ranch and Ennis, and they spent the night there. Each trip was a major undertaking with a horse-drawn wagon.

In any case, my first year in school was dismal and I looked forward only to the day when school would be out in the spring and I could return to the ranch. Such thoughts helped to sustain me during this difficult period.

Spring came at last and my parents came to get me. The road back up to the ranch passes across broad, sagebrush-covered benchlands, dropping down at last to the river. Beyond the river at this point rises a natural stone wall or cliff nearly a hundred feet high.

When I saw this stone wall I knew that we were nearing the ranch and soon I could see, in the far distance, the great mountains rising above and beyond the home ranch. I noticed that there was still much snow on the higher peaks.

Arriving at the ranch, I at once went down to the pasture to find old Snoozer. He was winter-thin but had not forgotten me and I was pleased. To me it seemed that I had been gone for at least a century but I quickly took up life again, the only life that was real and had meaning.

My ranch duties began at once. First, I was delegated to ride the fences, making minor repairs where necessary. I did not mind this work; I was out on the range among the wild things I loved. Yellow mayflowers were springing up everywhere and, near some snowbanks, glacier lilies were pushing up their yellow blooms. Meadowlarks sang from the open forest glades and birds of other kinds were busily building nests. Among the most interesting of these were the magpies. Nearly as large as crows, they built large, covered nests in the willows. The round openings were located in the sides of the nests and I could rarely resist the temptation of climbing up and putting my hand into the nests to feel the large, smooth eggs.

High above the ranch house, on the right-hand butte, were two rows of castle-like cliffs that had a twenty-foot passage between them, almost like a street. Upon the stone faces of these cliffs the cliff swallows always built their clay nests. These birds are very gregarious; often there would be several hundred of their gourd-shaped nests located close together. Frequently I would climb up the mountain, a distance of five or six hundred feet, to watch the birds at work on their nests. Like

I often watched cliff swallows building their mud nests upon the cliffs above the ranch. The mud had to be air-lifted about five hundred feet above the river.

little darts they would sail far down to the river's margin for loads of mud or clay and then flutter up again to apply the building material to the nests. What laborious toil it was! By counting the pellets of hardened clay in a finished nest, I determined that more than a hundred trips down to the river had been necessary for its completion.

After regurgitating her beakful of mud upon the edge of the nest under construction, a swallow would spiral downward toward the far-off river, her small form quickly disappearing, swallowed up by the distance. About fifteen minutes later she would return and flutter up to her nest and apply her mud to it. Sometimes she would then rest in the half-completed nest for a few minutes; at other times she would leave at once for another load. The work of building one of these nests was prodigious when one considers the great height to which the mud had to be air-lifted.

Several miles above the ranch, there were some cliffs along the river where the swallows also nested. These swallows had it

much easier, since they built their nests only about thirty feet
from good sources of mud. This place was known as Swallow
Cliffs and was a favorite place for trout fishing.

Cliff swallows also took advantage of the ranch buildings as
nesting sites; they built their nests under the protection of overhanging eaves. Several times they tried to nest under the eaves
of the ranch house, but their nests were always knocked off by
my father, who said that they carried lice.

One of their favored nesting sites was the horse barn where,
to my delight, I found that I could climb up into the hayloft
and peek out under the eaves to watch the birds at work. In this
way my eyes were only inches away from the birds as they
toiled. I could watch as the semiliquid mud was forced from
their beaks upon the edges of the nests. While working, the
birds emitted low chirping sounds as though they were singing
at their work. I never tired of watching them and my nearness
never appeared to bother them.

The sudden arrival of summer brought numerous other birds.
From warm southern climes came bluebirds, robins, and other
small birds. After summer showers the robins sang their cheer-
up songs and I listened entranced to their joyous voices.

Located in the middle of the river below the ranch buildings
there was a small willow-covered island, perhaps twenty feet
long and half as wide. A pair of Canada geese always nested
there, frequently coming across to feed upon the clover in our
lower pasture. They were voracious feeders, often denuding a
large area along the river. Out on the island I could sometimes
see their heads bobbing up and down above the tall grass.
Later, I watched fluffy goslings swimming about in the quiet
water below the island. My vantage point was in the dense
growth of sagebrush near the river's edge.

A short distance above the ranch, along the river, there was a
low area fringed by a dense growth of tall pines and many
willows. At its center was a small lake where a family of beav-

ers always lived. They had constructed their stick houses near one end of the lake and I frequently watched as they swam, their heads just breaking the surface, making ripple rings that spread away. Muskrats also inhabited the lake.

Just above this small body of water there was an area covered with very tall pines in which a large number of great blue herons nested, their large stick nests located more than fifty feet above the ground. Often I would sit on the hillside above the little lake listening to them. They were very noisy birds, making loud raucous sounds that could be heard for a great distance. I suppose these noises were emitted by the hungry young while being fed. Since there were many nests, the confused racket reminded me of a distant dogfight. It went on all day, with the adult herons leaving and returning to the nests with food for their voracious offspring. Once I attempted to climb up to one of the nests, but was foiled by height and inaccessibility. The herons, I decided, had known what they were doing when they had chosen these tall trees as nesting places.

This was one of the summers that White Bear and his family came to camp at the ranch. White Bear was a Crow Indian and each summer he left the reservation in eastern Montana and went camping. In addition to his squaw, he had two teen-age sons and a small child. The sons were named Red Bear and Yellow Bear. Upon arriving at the ranch, they set up their tepee down along the river and later came up to the house to trade for elk and deerskins.

We always had a number of skins from elk and deer killed by my father and other men at the ranch. These were traded to White Bear for tanned leather gloves, usually about two pairs of gloves per skin. White Bear took the skins down to the tepee and the next morning I could see his squaw out in the river tramping upon the skins with her bare feet. This was to soften them up. In my spare time I often went down and sat by the

small fire in the tepee watching the tanning process. After
being well soaked in the river, wood ashes were rubbed on the
hair side. This loosened the hair, which was then rubbed off.
The next step, I found, was smearing beef brains on the skins.
Steers were periodically being slaughtered at the ranch and so
beef brains were usually available. This oily material made the
skins very soft and pliable, and they were then worked over a
rounded board driven into the ground. The final step was placing the softened skins over a low willow fire. I am not sure of
the reason for this latter step, but it did give the skins a russet
color and a most pleasing scent. The resulting material closely
resembled chamois skin and was then ready for making into
gloves or moccasins.

The gloves when finished were of excellent quality, beauti-
fully made. They were the standard work gloves worn by all
the men at the ranch.

White Bear was elderly by Indian standards, but very spry.
His squaw, of course, did almost all of the work of wood gathering, cooking, and glovemaking. Before the arrival of whites in
the area White Bear had participated in Indian wars. Often, at
night, I walked down and sat in the tepee listening to the
talk, little of which I understood, since it was mostly in Indian.
Even in midsummer there was a mountain chill and so a small
fire always burned at the center of the tepee, the smoke flowing
out of the smoke hole at the top. The child would always be
laced in its cradleboard propped against the wall.

White Bear could speak English when necessary and, one
night, I asked him if he had ever been in any old Indian battles.
He replied that he had been. "Once," he said, "we have big war
over near Red Rock Lake. Fought for three days."

"How many Indians were killed?" I asked.

Very seriously, he said, "Kill one man."

Later, when I told my grandfather about White Bear's state-
ment, he commented that the one casualty had probably oc-

curred when the Indian's horse had stumbled into a badger hole! These battles, I gathered, were rather similar to modern football games, with the squaws and children whooping it up in encouragement from the surrounding hillsides like a rooting section.

Bread was baked about once a week at the ranch and one of these bakings did not turn out well. This was the second week after White Bear's arrival. Thinking that the Indians would not know the difference, the entire batch of bread was given to them. The next day, my father encountered White Bear out in the mountains. They were both on horseback and as soon as they were within speaking distance, White Bear asked, "What kind of flour make bad bread?"

White Bear and his family remained at the ranch all the rest of the summer. He put it this way, "Heap visit; all the time visit."

When autumn came, the Indians hooked up their buckboard wagon and left, returning to the reservation for the winter. White Bear's squaw had not had time to finish making all the gloves bargained for, but he said that she would make them and he would send them to us. About Christmas a letter was received from White Bear, written by the Indian Agent, saying that his squaw had died but that as soon as he got another squaw he would send the gloves. We never got them. Presumably, good squaws were hard to come by.

Old White Bear has long since gone to the Happy Hunting Grounds, but I recall with pleasure the nights I sat in his tepee beside the tiny fire, listening enthralled to the conversations. I see again the dim shadows of the Indians projected upon the walls by the flickering flames and hear once more the rippling sounds of the flowing river just outside in the dark, mysterious mountain night.

During the summer I had very carefully refrained from asking what month it was or how soon I would have to go away to school. School, to me, was still a dirty word, and I figured that if I kept quiet the whole idea would go away like a bad dream. However, one day in late August, when autumn was definitely in the air, my father informed me that I could remain at the ranch during the coming winter if I would consent to being taught by my mother and would attend to my studies. Naturally, this was wonderful news and I agreed to study very hard. I would have agreed to anything.

A week later the weather turned cold and, in the morning, when I looked up at the high mountains, their tops were white with snow. Winter was on the way and, this time, I was glad.

2

DEEP WINTER

ONE MORNING in mid-September when I looked out of my cabin window I saw that the ground was white with new-fallen snow. This first snow was fluffy and clung to the twigs of the trees and to the dead weeds and grasses; not a breath of air stirred in the white world. This first winter snow, I knew, would melt as soon as the sun came out, but it was a forerunner of much more to come. The closing-down of winter in the high Rockies is much more significant than the arrival of winter in warmer climes, and a person who has never experienced it can have no conception of its impact. On a cattle ranch such as ours there are many preparations that must be made. Sheds for cattle must be made ready to care for livestock as well as adequate supplies of hay. As usual, the timothy and clover hay had been harvested and stacked. Grain for the hogs and chickens had to be threshed and stored. Large amounts of firewood had to be cut. The only woods available were aspen and pine, soft woods that burned quickly, giving out great heat but burning rapidly. Everything had to be carefully planned or disaster could result.

All these preparations for winter had already been started. A pile of stovewood, nearly as large as the ranch house, was

Winter begins on the high mountains and, day by day, the snow creeps downward. This is an early winter snow.

stacked nearby, and the cattle had been rounded up and driven down to the ranch area near the sheds. These sheds were, of necessity, very warm, having been insulated by wheat straw. They consisted of jack pine poles spiked to both sides of ten-inch posts, with wheat straw jammed down between them. Later, when temperatures dropped to twenty-five degrees or even forty degrees below zero, I was always amazed at how warm the sheds were. The body heat of the crowded cattle raised the temperature to a very comfortable point.

Farther down the valley was a large cattle ranch operated by a well-known circus concern. They used discarded circus tents to house their livestock, but I often wondered about the protection they afforded, since a tent is about the coldest shelter possible. The truth, of course, is that if cattle or horses are shielded from the wind they can survive in good condition. Cold winds suck away body heat and the animals may eventually succumb.

Little by little we prepared for the coming winter. Many of the wild animals, in their own way, were also getting ready. No longer did the marmots sun themselves upon the sun-warmed boulders; they slept the deep sleep of hibernation in snug dens in the earth. So did the ground squirrels. Only the flesh-eaters were active. Along the river I saw the tracks of mink and, at night, I heard the howls of coyotes drifting down from the surrounding bluffs. Everywhere, in the new snow, were the tracks of jack rabbits, about the only small plant-eaters that remained active in the snow.

When the sun came out, temperatures rose; this first autumn snow quickly melted and the ground was again bare. The early snowfall had been but a foretaste of things to come, a warning, I suppose, to the creatures of the wild mountains to make ready.

High up on the mountain range above the ranch, the snow did not melt. It was already winter up there, and the deer and elk that had grazed on the exposed slopes all summer began moving down into the valleys.

It was at this time that we had our yearly invasion of pack rats. Apparently seeking warm places for the winter, they entered the ranch house and storage buildings in large numbers, even during the daytime. One afternoon, as I sat on the back porch peeling potatoes for my mother I spotted a large pack rat along the wall. Emulating the skill of one of the cowhands, a Mexican, I had been practicing knife-throwing, and so I threw the butcher knife at the rat, pinning it to the floor. I was as surprised as the rat. In any case, my mother came out of the kitchen as a result of the sound and was most unhappy at my use of her favorite kitchen knife. She discarded the knife and never used it again.

The nights were becoming colder and I often listened to the honking of wild geese passing high overhead in the darkness. I

marveled that they could find their way across the vast mountain ranges. The robins and most other small birds had already
gone south, but a few, including chickadees, remained. Clark's
nutcrackers—we called them camp robbers—appeared, probably from the higher elevations where they had nested. These
latter birds would remain with us all through the long winter,
becoming tamer and tamer as the season progressed.

To my sorrow my parents decided that I should move into
the ranch house for the winter. My cottage had no heat and so
it was no doubt a good idea. In the house I had an upstairs
room with a window that looked out across the distant river
and the mountains beyond. I was not too unhappy.

I still rode and walked my usual trails in the mountains, but
no longer could I hunt "bugs" or study the local flora. However,
I visited a warm spring on the ranch where there were many
aquatic plants and insects. I found some flat-sided jars in a store
room into which I placed some of the aquatic specimens.
Through the walls of these "aquaria" I could watch the activities of caddis insects and water beetles. I was especially
fascinated by the caddis insects, watching how they built their
cases of bright pebbles. I thought that it would be interesting
to remove all the sand and pebbles from my aquaria and substitute small colored beads from my mother's sewing basket. I
visualized them constructing cases of these pretty beads, but
the caddises would not cooperate and so I was forced to supply
them with their usual sand and pebbles.

By the middle of October it had become much colder and the
snow line had day by day crept down the slopes of the mountains. When I rode up on the bench above the ranch I could see
that the Dead Man Creek area was white with snow. This was
real winter snow and would remain all winter.

By now great piles of firewood had been cut. This wood was
cut with crosscut, two-man saws; unfortunately, chain saws
were far in the future. Our woodpile, however, was smaller

Cutting wood for winter. Large amounts of stove wood had to be cut to last until spring.

than the one down at the home ranch of my grandparents. They had a larger house, more bunkhouses, and thus more stoves.

The final preparation for winter isolation was the laying in of food supplies. This, of course, required a trip down to Chowning's grocery store at Ennis, forty miles away. It was a four-day trip by wagon, two down and two back. The modern housewife who goes grocery shopping several times a week can have no conception of the problems related to planning and buying five months' supplies. Everything had to be bought in large quantities—fifty-pound sacks of flour, large bags of sugar, as well as a variety of canned goods by the case. Not only would our own supplies be bought but enough for the home ranch and those needed by West Fork Kelly and other neighbors.

We took off on a cold early winter day. There was light snow on the ground, but the occasional mud puddles were not yet frozen. By late afternoon we reached my uncle's ranch near Cameron where the night was spent. Around the fire that evening I listened entranced to the tales recounted by my father and Uncle Keller. They had both come west with my grandparents in the eighties. Travel had been by covered wagon and the hardships they endured were amazing. However, looking back, they seemed to find humor in most everything that had happened along the way, from encounters with grizzly bears in the mountains to floods along the Platte River.

Uncle Keller decided to go along with us down to Ennis for his own supplies and, upon our arrival at Chowning's store, we went in and began picking out what was needed. These supplies made a large pile and we then began loading them into the two wagons. Uncle Keller was wearing a long buffalo coat that reached nearly to the floor. After he had paid for his supplies, he remarked to Mr. Chowning, "Looks like you would give me a few of those nice apples in that box there, considering the money we have spent."

Mr. Chowning then told him, "That's fine, Mr. Keller. You just fill up your pocket."

What Mr. Chowning didn't know was that the pockets of Uncle Keller's coat had no inner linings. He began putting apples into one of the coat pockets. Finally, Mr. Chowning remarked, "My, my, Mr. Keller, you certainly do have big pockets."

Uncle Keller continued to drop apples into his pocket. The apples, of course, were falling down between the outer buffalo skin and the inner lining of the coat. At last Uncle Keller walked out of the store, barely able to stagger under the weight of nearly half a box of apples.

I rode with Uncle Keller back up to Cameron and he chuckled all the way. It had not been the free apples he had gotten but the fun of fleecing the storekeeper. I was a great admirer of

Cutting ice for summer. Note blocks at center. This ice was stored in an icehouse insulated with sawdust, and would last all summer.

Uncle Keller; he was always up to some trick. I liked to hear him tell about his experiences while freighting supplies through what is now Yellowstone Park. Grizzly bears were often a problem and the only way he could find to chase them away from his camps at night was through the use of Roman candles. The bears couldn't stand them.

Uncle Keller had eventually settled near Cameron at Bear Creek. All had gone well until another settler arrived and settled about eight miles away down the valley. This made it far too crowded for Uncle Keller and so he had gone to Alaska during the 1898 gold rush. There he had found the panning of gold in the sand and gravels of the Yukon too laborious and too much of a gamble. So he and a partner had acquired dog teams and began hauling potatoes into the interior where the miners were willing to pay twenty-five dollars per pound for them, sprouts and all. This was the only fresh vegetable food obtainable to ward off scurvy during the long arctic winters. This business was far more lucrative than scrabbling in the creeks for elusive gold.

Meanwhile, back at the ranch, as TV westerns say, the supplies obtained at Ennis were stowed away for the winter. There was a cellar at the ranch that had been dug into the side of the mountain back of the ranch house. It consisted of inner walls of pine logs covered with five or six feet of earth. There were thick, double doors. Inside this cellar the temperature never dropped to freezing and so almost all foods stored there remained safe all winter, even when the outside temperature fell far below zero. This included various vegetables grown at the ranch as well as canned goods.

In late autumn, after most of the ranch work had been finished, my father and the other men at the ranch went hunting. Game animals were abundant in the mountains and a number of elk, deer, and mountain sheep were killed and brought back to the ranch. We had a screened enclosure about ten feet square in which the carcasses were suspended. They quickly froze solid and constituted our winter's meat supply. A meat saw was kept in this enclosure and all we had to do was saw off steaks and roasts as needed. Thus, we had the forerunner of the electric deep freezer.

People from the East often asked what we ate during the long mountain winters. We usually told them that, in the fall, we made a large washtub full of soup and put it out to freeze. Whenever we wanted soup we just chopped out a chunk with an axe and thawed it out. Simple! This was supposed to be a joke, yet this is approximately what we do today in using frozen foods from a home freezer.

The climate of the high Montana Rockies is almost arctic in severity. It was not at all unusual for the thermometer to fall to forty or fifty below zero within a few hours. West Yellowstone, twenty miles away and at a higher elevation than the ranch, has since experienced temperatures of seventy degrees below. Thus, the local winter climate is not too much different than that of Alaska. By contrast, some coastal Alaskan towns, such as Juno, warmed by the Japan Current, rarely experience temperatures much below minus twenty degrees Fahrenheit.

After the trip to Ennis, things at the ranch settled down to a routine. Each morning the cattle had to be fed hay and the watering holes had to be chopped free of ice which had frozen over during the previous night. The snow continued to fall and by mid-November lay nearly a yard deep on the level ground. Rim ice formed along the margin of the river, in some places extending out ten feet or more. About the only means of travel now was by skis. This was not by any means a mere sport but a serious means of transportation. Some of our skis had been made at the ranch, others were factory-made. My own skis, shorter than those used by the men, had been locally constructed of pine. Their tips had been curved upward after being steamed in a washboiler and then allowed to dry on a rack. To

My sister Lucille and I on skis at the ranch. To us these skis were a means of transportation, not a sport.

make them slick we used paraffin, applied with a flatiron. The best wax, however, consisted of old broken Edison phonograph records. These records were cylindrical in form and made of hard wax that lasted a long while when applied to the skis.

We usually called these items of travel "snowshoes" but they were, of course, not snowshoes. These latter contrivances are webbed and resemble tennis rackets in a general way. True snowshoes are used in regions where the snow remains soft and powdery, having no hard crust on the surface. In our region, the midday sun usually melted the surface, which then froze hard at night. For this reason, skis could slide quickly over it and a man could cover long distances in a single day. Travel by snowshoes, on the other hand, is a slow, plodding process. On skis, a man, at each "step," may slide ten or more feet over hard snow on level ground.

While we often slid down mountainsides for several miles, we never attempted gymnastics and so never sustained injuries. I never heard of a broken bone from skiing until it became a fancy sport.

Needless to say, we had few visitors in winter; we were too far off the beaten track. It was a big occasion when West Fork Kelly skied down for conversation and a meal. On one of these visits he was greatly embarrassed when he bit into a cream puff and it shot him in the eye. He never lived it down.

There were a few other bachelors from back in the mountains who sometimes came to the ranch. The usual custom was for them to come in and sit down for supper, unannounced and unexpected. Guests were always welcome.

By December, winter had really settled down. When I looked up toward the high mountains back of the ranch I could usually see them draped with cold mist that streamed away from the peaks like smoke. The land was in the tight grip of winter, but we had prepared for it and lived snug in the log ranch house. My sister and I were forced to attend to our lessons, but our mother was not very strict, which suited me fine. My sister, Lucille, four years younger than I, was content to remain indoors but I still found outside activities more to my liking.

In the severe climate, it was not unusual for one of the cattle to die. When this occurred the remains would be dragged off to some remote spot and several coyote traps set around it. In addition to the beautiful coyote skins, which had considerable value, the state paid a bounty for the destruction of the beasts. This was sponsored by the Cattlemen's Association.

One of my jobs this winter was visiting these carcasses to see if any coyotes had been caught. One dead steer had been dragged up the river for about five miles. This was not far from the mouth of the canyon, the place where the Madison River emerged from the Madison Range.

One of these trips stands out in my memory. On this day the weather was clear, the sun shining brightly upon the snow, causing it to sparkle as if covered with a million diamonds. The temperature was near zero that afternoon as I put on my skis, picked up my gun, and took off up the river.

Within half a mile I passed the swamp where the family of beavers lived. The little lake was, of course, frozen over now and the ice was covered with a foot of snow. I skied across the lake to the beaver house and tapped on it with one of my ski poles. As I expected, there was a loud splash from beneath my feet as the animals hit the water. Each time I passed the place I could not resist the temptation of worrying the beavers a little. Secure beneath the frozen lake surface, they lived throughout the winter, feeding upon the bark of aspen limbs stored there in autumn. Most of their time in winter was spent resting in the den inside their stick house, just above the water's level. Whenever alarmed, they would plunge into the water and swim away.

Continuing on, I passed the heron rookery, now deserted. The noisy birds had long since reared their young and gone south, but their large nests could still be seen high up in the trees.

Emerging from the swamp area, I came eventually to a level bench stretching as far as I could see. The sunlight upon the snow was almost blinding as I skied out onto the bench where there was not a vestige of any vegetation. Even the tall sagebrushes now lay buried under the unbroken snow and not a living thing moved in the vast expanse spreading out before me. It was truly a frozen world. Far above, to the left, rose the mountain range, glistening white in the winter sun.

My skis slid smoothly over the hard, crusted snow. I was a small boy almost lost in the immensity of the cold, white landscape. I hurried on, squinting my eyes against the glare. At last I reached the end of the bench and coasted down a gentle slope to the river where a warm spring emerged from the hillside. As I approached the open spring, there was a sudden flutter of wings as a duck flew up and sailed out across the river. It was one of the few ducks that spent the winter in the area, enabled to do so by living and feeding in the waters of the warm spring.

Just beyond the spring was the carcass of the steer. There were no coyotes in the traps, but half a dozen camp robbers sat upon the carcass, driving their beaks into the frozen flesh. To me there was something wild and primitive in the scene, a throwback to the feral and savage ways of the wild mountains.

Thoughtfully, I turned my skis around and followed my tracks back toward the ranch. The sun had by then dropped down behind the mountains to the left, but the tips of the higher mountains to my right were still tinged with a reddish glow. Overhead rode a full moon, becoming brighter as the gloom down in the valley increased. I hurried home and as I passed the frozen swamp I heard the howl of a coyote, lonely and elemental. It was a call of the wild, the voice of a lonely place. Chills ran up my spine and I was glad when I, at last, saw the comforting lights of the ranch house in the distance.

Later that night, as I lay in bed beneath layers of heavy blankets, I again heard coyote howls—this time, several of them, drifting down from the surrounding mountains, repeated again and again as the beasts sang their eerie songs upon the far, windswept ridges under the moon. Deep within my being there stirred strange longings to learn and to know more about the wild land in which I lived but which I did not understand. I slept at last, while the outside cold penetrated the unheated room.

A couple of nights later we were seated in the living room near the wood fire. It was long after dark and it was very cold outside. Suddenly there was a loud knock at the door, a most unusual occurrence in deep winter. My father opened the door to reveal a strange apparition. Only after this ghost—or whatever it was—had entered and approached the lamplight did it dawn on me that it was a large woman dressed in well-padded coveralls.

The woman turned out to be none other than Six-Shooter Sal, a notorious character of the mountains. I had heard wild tales about her, but had never seen her before. She warmed herself at the fire while telling us her story. She lived about twenty miles up the river and had walked down, following the river's rim ice in the subzero weather. She wished to spend the night. Now western hospitality could be strained to a great extent but not that far.

After warming herself, she unbuttoned the drop-seat of her coveralls, revealing a number of inner pockets containing various items, including a packet of photographs and a 38-caliber revolver. I had heard that she was as nutty as a fruitcake and the items she carried confirmed the stories.

My father informed Six-Shooter Sal that every bed at the ranch was occupied and told her that he would hitch up a team and take her down to the next ranch about eight miles farther down the valley. Very reluctantly, she finally agreed to this and it was done, much to my mother's relief.

Later we heard that the next ranch, in turn, had taken her on down to another ranch where she finally spent the night—what there was left of it.

Six-Shooter Sal had once had a husband, but he had left her. According to reports, she had shot a couple of men, killing none of them, through no fault of her own.

The following summer an uncle and I were up in the area where the old gal lived. Beside the road, behind a barbed-wire fence, there was a small tent with a hand-painted sign attached. The sign said, "First Aid to the Injured."

We looked inside the tent and saw that it contained only an old army cot. Then, looking beyond the tent, we could just see the ridgepole of Six-Shooter Sal's cabin above a sagebrush-covered ridge. Suddenly, she appeared on the cabin roof, waving a Winchester rifle about and looking in our direction. Needless to say, we took off like scalded Indians on our horses; we figured that she was fixing to create some ready-made patients for her clinic. I do not know what ever happened to Six-Shooter Sal and do not really care. Like Calamity Jane, she was a product of her time and place. Perhaps she was merely rushing women's lib a little. In any case, she was mean as a yard dog from all accounts.

This winter was unusually severe, with deep snows and plunging temperatures. Several times in December the thermometer registered forty-five degrees below zero. The ranch house was built of heavy pine logs which afforded excellent insulation, but when the weather became extremely frigid, frost began forming along the upper portions of the walls. It was not necessary to go outside to look at the thermometer; when the frost appeared on the walls we knew that it was below minus forty. When an outside door was opened a person could not see

Deep winter at the home ranch. This snow lasted from October until late March. It was more than three feet deep in most places.

out because of the steam. Fires had to be kept burning all night, and one could hear the timbers of the house snapping and popping due to the contraction of the wooden beams. When out in a pine forest, similar sounds were not uncommon as the trunks of the trees contracted in the cold.

My natural history studies had slowed down with the advent of winter, except for observations of the winter birds and animals. Often I skied down along the river, seeing many evidences of the nocturnal activities of wild creatures. Now and then, in the snow, I saw the tracks of weasels and rabbits. In many instances, I spotted the tiny trails of mice and the holes where they had come up out of the snow to run about.

We had a few head of sheep on the ranch, and one morning

My father with the mountain lion he killed on Christmas eve. The horse is my horse, Snoozer, the only one that would tolerate the large cat on its back.

the half-eaten remains of one of them was discovered near the barn. Around it were the tracks of a mountain lion. The tracks led away from the barn and up the mountainside above the ranch house.

It was the day before Christmas and my father took his Winchester down from the rack by the kitchen door and followed the lion tracks up the mountainside. I watched attentively from the kitchen window. Near the top of the pine-covered butte he disappeared into the timber, but I continued to watch. I had about lost interest after nearly an hour when he reappeared, now on the opposite side of the canyon near the Swallow Cliffs.

I could see that he was crouching low, his gun at the ready. Then I spotted a movement among the rocks below him and, a few moments later, the mountain lion walked into full view. Even at that distance I could tell that it was a magnificent animal. Father evidently saw the cat at about the same time. I could see the recoil of his gun, and, a second or so later, heard the sound of the shot. The lion leaped into the air and then rolled down the mountainside, coming to rest among some large boulders.

My father approached the cat very cautiously, as I could see from my vantage point. I knew that it was dead when he reached down and dragged it out onto the boulder.

It was no trouble getting the lion down to the house, since the steep mountainside was covered with crusted snow over which it could easily be dragged. The cat was unusually large, measuring nine feet from its nose to the tip of its tail. Certainly we would have had less sheep by spring if the animal had not been destroyed.

In recounting the lion hunt, my father said that the tracks led up the mountainside and into the pines where it had apparently spent much time in a hollowed-out boulder where it could watch the ranch, and, presumably, the sheep. No doubt it had also watched my sister and me in the back yard where we frequently practiced on our skis.

In later years I had several encounters with mountain lions. Once I rode up the trail along Papoose Creek and, when I returned, saw the tracks of a mountain lion in my horse tracks in the soft earth. Probably the cat had followed along behind me, stepping aside and hiding in a thicket when I had returned down the trail. This was not an unusual occurrence but, at the time, it gave me a queer feeling to realize that such a large beast had, indeed, been following me.

Later this same winter—I think it was in late January—my father dragged me away from my studies, not a difficult pro-

cess, and took me up to Dead Man Gulch. The day was sunny
and bright and our skis slipped lightly over the crusted snow.
Near the base of the mountain we came to an open glade surrounded by aspens, now bare of leaves. Upon entering the open
glade we were suddenly confronted by a strange scene. The
remains of a large deer lay in the snow, which was splattered
with blood. Investigation showed that the deer had been killed
by a mountain lion, the evidence being in the tracks in the
snow. Bit by bit we were able to piece the story together. We
found where the cat had crouched down behind a large fallen
log watching the deer. When the deer had come near enough,
the cat had sprung upon its back and ridden it for several hundred feet before bringing it down. The story of the kill was
clearly etched in the snow, and in my mind's eye I can still see
the quiet glade with its evidence of the life and death struggle.
Strangely, it disturbed me deeply, even though I realized that it
was the normal course of events in the wild, that there are
always the hunters and the hunted.

Strange things often happened in the wild area where our
ranch was located. One such instance occurred in the eighties,
shortly after my grandparents had settled there. One winter
morning my grandfather was aroused by the barking of the
dogs. He discovered that a wolflike beast of dark color was
chasing my grandmother's geese. He fired his gun at the animal
but missed. It ran off down the river, but several mornings later
it was again seen at about dawn. It was seen several more times
at the home ranch as well as at other ranches ten or fifteen
miles down the valley. Whatever it was, it was a great traveler.

Those who got a good look at the beast described it as being
nearly black and having high shoulders and a back that sloped
downward like that of a hynea. Then, one morning in late January, my grandfather was alerted by the dogs, and this time he
was able to kill it.

Just what the animal was is still an open question. After

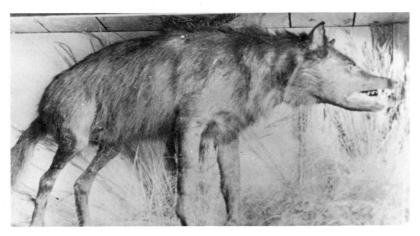

This is the strange beast killed at the ranch in the eighties. It has never been identified. Is it part hyena?

being killed, it was donated to a man named Sherwood who maintained a combination grocery and museum at Henry's Lake over in Idaho. It was mounted and displayed there for many years. He called it a "ringdocus." Later, Sherwood's collection of mounted animals was moved to West Yellowstone, where it was displayed for the edification of the tourists.

As a biologist, I have often wondered what the beast actually was. Was it, as some theorized, a hyena escaped from a circus? The nearest circus was hundreds of miles away. Ringdocus was just another mystery of the mountains, probably never to be solved.

The rest of this winter was relatively uneventful. Blizzards came and went and by February the snow lay deep upon the level ground. The snow had drifted up against the walls of the ranch house, giving it great insulation.

The dogs at the ranch were of various breeds. They were cattle dogs and, as such, never allowed into the house. When their food was taken out to them in the mornings, they could never be seen. However, when called, Old Ring and the rest would pop up out of the drifted snow where they had buried

Cross-country travel was often by dog teams. The dogs were of various breeds.

themselves against the cold. Not far removed from their counterparts, the wolves, they knew how to take care of themselves. They were vicious brutes and often fought savagely among themselves. Sometimes one of them would be killed. It was a cruel land and, like the people who dwelled there, the dogs had to adapt in order to survive.

To me, one of the most peculiar things occurred at about this time. There was a snowdrift nearly six feet deep, between the water hole and the barns in which both cattle and horses were kept. A narrow passage nearly a hundred feet long had been shoveled through this drift to enable the livestock to get from one location to the other. On the morning in question, ten head of cattle had met an equal number of saddle horses at the center of the cut. There they stood, looking at each other, neither side willing nor knowing how to back up. The passage was too narrow to allow them to pass each other. Things were at a deadlock when the situation was discovered by one of the ranch hands.

At first the men attempted to back up the saddle horses, but a saddle horse apparently does not know how to back up; it is not a part of its training. A cow will not or cannot back up, and so things were at a standoff.

Now this may not seem to be a complicated situation, but it was. It took most of the day to dig the passage wide enough to allow the beasts to pass each other.

By this time I was tired of winter and longed for spring, when I could again roam the mountain trails. Sometimes, of course, I skied away from the ranch, looking for whatever was to be seen. Several times, on sunny days, I spotted large patches of snowfleas on the surface of the snow. These patches of tiny insects were usually about a yard across and so covered the snow as to make it appear almost black. When I waved my ski pole near them, the cluster moved away, remaining together as a group.

Snowfleas are among the strangest of insects. I read about them in some of my books and found that they were actually springtails or Collembolas, not fleas at all. They come up through the snow on sunny days, retreating down to the under-lying earth at night. I had a small hand lens and was able to study their jumping mechanisms in detail. Beneath their bodies are springing organs, fitting into catches. When these organs were released the small insects were propelled through the air. How, I wondered, were these little insects able to remain active when all other insects were hibernating or passing the winter as eggs?

Warmer weather came in late March and the snow began melting. Water ran from beneath the drifts and down the hill-sides. Chunks of rim ice along the river tore loose and floated downstream. The snow was now wet and soggy, not fit for ski-ing. A few spring birds appeared and, one day, I spotted a robin. Spring was, at last, on the way.

I now obtained permission to move back into my own cabin where I could do as I pleased and be among my specimens. Just beyond the back window I was delighted to find that a robin was already building her nest, even though there was still plenty of snow on the ground. It seemed to me that she was rushing the season a little, but I supposed that she knew what she was doing. In any case, I decided to watch her and see how she made out. A few days later I could see four blue eggs in the nest. That night it snowed, and when I looked out in the morning the robin sat quietly on her nest, almost completely covered with fluffy snow. This was the last snow of the season and I am happy to report that my robin brought her nesting efforts to a successful conclusion in spite of climatic hazards.

It was spring once more in the high Rockies. Living things revived and became active again. Alpine flowers opened their blooms and trees unfolded new leaves. Marmots reappeared upon the great boulders down in the meadow, absorbing the heat of the sun after spending the cold months in hibernation. It was a time of reawakening, of rebirth. The living forces of the high Rockies were stirring again in a cycle as old as the mountains themselves, and I thrilled to the calls of returning birds and to the warm winds blowing down the valley.

It was a land bound neither by city blocks nor trimmed hedges. It was big beyond the petty dimensions of space, a land where the eye could sweep from the crests of snow-crowned mountains down to the rivers surging far below. It was a land that was either loved or hated by those who dwelled there. To some, the mountains seemed like prison walls, but to me they offered a secure haven where I was at home with the wild creatures and plant life I was gradually learning to appreciate and to understand.

3
DAYS OF SPRING AND SUMMER

SPRING COMES quickly and unannounced in the high Rockies. Almost overnight the snow turns soft and begins to melt. As the sun warms the mountains, the great banks of snow along the high ridges become waterlogged and eventually break away, sliding down the steep slopes, tearing off great trees and carrying along large boulders intermingled with splintered limbs and trunks. These snowslides are among Nature's great cataclysms, powerful almost beyond belief. They may completely denude an entire mountainside, rushing down into valleys and canyons. We often heard their rumbling sounds from distant mountains on sunny spring days. I recall reading in the journals of the Lewis and Clark expedition that, while passing through Montana in spring, they heard rumbling sounds they attributed to distant cannon fire. There were, of course, no cannons in Montana at that time and so the sounds they heard were certainly the deep rumblings of far-off snowslides.

One spring a great snowslide thundered down the mountainside near the mouth of the Madison Canyon, out of which the river passes about six miles upriver from the ranch. We distinctly heard the sound. A couple of hours later we noticed that the bed of the river was practically dry, the great boulders in it exposed. Something very unusual had happened, but we did not then know what. Then, a couple of hours later, with a great rumbling, the water rushed down its bed again, carrying dead trees and driftwood. It was later discovered that the snowslide near the mouth of the canyon had completely blocked the river, damming up its waters for several hours. Later, when the snow dam broke, the accumulated water had rushed down the valley in a flood, carrying everything before it. This great snowslide took place at almost the same spot where the disastrous earthquake of 1959 was to occur in which twenty-nine people were killed and buried forever beneath the millions of cubic yards of stone and earth. That, however, is another story to be recounted later.

Probably the first real sign of spring at the ranch was when one of the cowpunchers would come riding down out of the

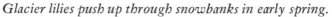
Glacier lilies push up through snowbanks in early spring.

Bird-bills or shooting stars (Dodecatheon) *are common flowers in the mountains.*

mountains proudly carrying a large bunch of glacier lilies in his hand. He would present these to my mother who would place them in a vase. Certainly such an incident has no resemblance to the character of the Western cowpokes as portrayed on television screens of today. On Saturday nights in town they might shoot out lights while riding down the street, but otherwise they were mostly a very human breed of men and I grew up admiring and riding with them. Often they married the local schoolmarm and settled down in tarpaper shacks to rear families. They homesteaded parcels of land and became the backbone of Western culture.

The snow continued to melt and flowers sprang up as if by magic. There were shooting stars—we called them bird-bills—buttercups or mayflowers, and numerous others. Yellow glacier lilies, impatient for spring, pushed up through the snow along the margins of receding snowbanks. The quaking aspens unfolded disc-shaped leaves that trembled in the sun and the willows along the streams expanded their catkins. This was my favorite time for roaming the mountains either afoot or on horseback. I was interested in everything concerning the wild area—the flowers, the forests, the wild animals, and the insects. Back of the ranch was a deep canyon with steep buttes rising on either side. Up the side of the left-hand butte ran a trail leading up to a level sagebrush-covered bench. This level bench stretched back to the high mountain range, a distance of perhaps two miles.

On one May afternoon I took off on my horse, climbing up the trail. Now, looking back, I am rather amazed that I was never required to report my intentions or destinations to my parents. I suppose they assumed me to be capable of taking care of myself. Life in such a frontier region appears to breed self-reliance, and self-reliance is expected.

On this particular day I went up the trail looking at everything along the way. Always there was something different to be seen or ruminated about. The trail finally led up out of the canyon and meandered among sagebrushes almost as high as my horse. Looking off to the left I noticed a bare ridge along which a large bank of winter snow remained. I reined in my horse and sat watching the scene spread out before me, the bench stretching away to the high mountains, still largely covered with snow, and ragged clouds hanging above their rugged peaks.

Suddenly my eyes were attracted by a slight movement on the distant ridge. Then a lone coyote walked into full view, posed against the sky, looking in my direction. The coyote's movements were unhurried and unafraid; apparently it assumed that I presented no threat to it. After a few seconds it trotted off and disappeared from view and I continued on up the trail. Meadowlarks called their plaintive notes from the distance and a hawk circled high against the clouds. The spring scene was quiet and very typical, and I was at peace with myself and the world around me.

At last the trail crossed Dead Man Creek where it flowed down across the prairie-like bench. Its banks were covered with moss and, here and there, small spring flowers were just opening their blooms. I dismounted and flopped down on my belly to drink the crystal-clear water. Then I sat for a minute or so on a large boulder surveying the surroundings. Meanwhile, my horse, not interested in the spring scene, munched the fresh grasses growing among the sagebrushes and boulders.

Some distance away I noticed a badger hole with freshly excavated earth beside it. As I watched, the flat head of a large badger appeared. It looked over the edge of the heap of earth, regarding me calmly through beady eyes. Like the coyote, it seemed unafraid, but regarded me with caution. Shortly, its head disappeared, then reappeared, this time less afraid. Soon it crawled out of its hole and hurried away through the surrounding sagebrush, perhaps to hunt for ground squirrels whose burrows were evident everywhere among the vegetation. The badger, I knew, could quickly dig out the hapless rodents and devour them, but it never occurred to me to feel sorry for the ground squirrels; they were merely a part of the wild nature I knew, each animal playing out its role in the scheme of things. Ethics had no part in it. A badger must live.

After the badger had vanished among the tall sagebrushes I remounted and rode leisurely on up the trail toward the distant mountains where cloud shadows drifted slowly across the slopes. I had no particular destination. Soon I passed near a dense growth of aspens. It was dark among the trees and I could see into them but a short distance. I reined my horse and sat quietly watching. Nothing moved, but I heard the scream of a hawk among the trees and overhead an eagle sailed on quiet wings. Suddenly I became conscious of another sound. It began as a low drumming, then rose in a crescendo, fading away at

In summer many alpine flowers bloom in the vicinity. In the meadow, down along a creek, were elephant-heads. They belong to the figwort family.

last into silence. Then it began again, and again faded away. This sound, I knew, was the drumming of a grouse. Once I had hidden and watched one of these birds beating its wings upon a dead tree trunk, and now I could picture it as it went through its mating ritual deep among the aspens.

The eagle sailed off beyond the trees and disappeared and I pulled at the reins, much to the disgust of my horse who, meantime, had been munching the succulent spring grass.

Shortly, the trail meandered near a cluster of old buildings, partly fallen into disrepair. Years before a family had settled here and attempted to make a living in the face of almost insurmountable odds. They had been defeated at last by a combination of factors, not the least of which had been the long winters when snows lay a yard deep upon the ground and temperatures often dropped far below zero. The settlers had eventually moved on to greener—and warmer—pastures, and only the old log buildings remained as evidences of a passing dream.

Beneath the ancient barn a groundhog had dug its den, and he now peered out at me with inquisitive eyes. Deciding that I meant him no harm, he crawled on out of his den and lay upon the sun-warmed mound of earth, watching as I rode on by.

Beyond the old cabins the trail followed along Dead Man Creek, but the creek itself was screened from view by dense growths of willows beneath which the ground was carpeted with new grass. As I came around a bend in the trail I surprised a large porcupine ambling along. It paid me no heed, moving leisurely into the willows. A porcupine has few enemies and so is unafraid. Like the skunk, its means of defense is extremely effective and it goes its way, refusing to be hurried. Near the point where I had seen the porcupine I noticed a large willow, almost completely stripped of bark. Here, I surmised, was where the porcupine had spent most of the previous winter, feeding upon the bark as is the way of porcupines.

The trail up Dead Man Creek was now approaching the base

Attractive bluebells (Campanula) *grow along Cascade Creek.*

of the mountains. It entered a growth of jack pines and crossed a marshy area where I spotted a number of elk tracks in the mud but saw none of the animals. Beyond the marsh was an open glade where my family often parked their wagons and ate picnic lunches while in search of the delicious huckleberries that grew there. I was very familiar with the surroundings and rode on up toward the base of the mountains which now rose far above me, their sides steep and barren of vegetation of any sort. The trail came to an abrupt end at the foot of a talus slope and my horse could go no farther. For awhile I sat in the saddle gazing up the mountainside where a few coneys, or pikas, perched on some of the larger boulders. Now and then they gave their cries, lonely and plaintive. Already, even though it was only spring, the coneys had been busy gathering their stores of hay; they had collected various kinds of vegetation and piled it beneath overhanging rocks to dry in the spring sun. Among the desiccated plants I could identify lupines, violets, and a few sprigs of grass.

These little rabbit-like creatures have counterparts in Asia and, in America, coneys range southward almost to Mexico. They dwell in remote canyons and mountainsides, apparently happy in habitats that are austere and inhospitable. Their voices are the voices of isolated and wild places, remote from the haunts of men. They are able to survive here only because of their habit of laying up stores of hay as winter food.

While observing the coneys I had been hunched over in the saddle, oblivious to the boulder-strewn slopes rising far above me. Now my eyes lifted up toward the jagged ramparts of the range where I saw the white forms of three bighorns moving slowly across the steep mountainside. Their white winter coloration made them stand out against the dark rocky slope. Later their coats would turn darker, but this early in the spring they still retained their white shade. Down at the ranch we had several Rocky Mountain bighorn skins, and visitors from the East were always surprised to see that they had hair instead of wool. I suppose they had assumed that all sheep had wool.

High above the three bighorns I saw a lone hawk circling on motionless wings. No doubt its eyes were focused upon the coneys far below, but I was certain that it was in vain. At the slightest hint of danger the alert little creatures would emit loud warning cries and dart down to safety among the tumbled boulders where no hawk could reach them.

This was the end of the trail and so I turned my horse and went back down into the open grassy glade, watching for signs of moose, bear, or elk, but all was silent except for the calls of a few birds. I turned toward the left and urged my horse up the hillside, passing through low-growing shrubs. Shortly, the land leveled off, covered with a dense growth of pines. We continued on with no specific destination in mind. Now and then I noticed mushrooms lodged high in the crotches of pine limbs. These, I knew, had been placed there by red squirrels as a sort of storage against times of need. The mushrooms were dry and would remain edible for a long while.

My meandering way led at last to a woodland lake, perhaps ten acres in extent. How or why it had been formed I could not guess. It had no inlet or outlet and its banks were green and mossy. Out in the center I could see a tiny island which looked intriguing, as islands usually do. I had visited the lake many times but had never set foot upon the island. A few dead leaves floated on the lake's mirror-like surface and, here and there, I noticed dead geometrid moths, their pale wings expanded upon the surface. The depth of the water appeared to be five or six feet, but I could see no fish. Probably it would have been impossible for fish to have gained access to the lake because it was remote from any stream. No doubt this sylvan lake had long ago been formed by the sinking of the area during an earthquake. Earthquakes are frequent in the vicinity; years later this area would be torn asunder by a violent quake and the place where my lake was situated would be almost totally destroyed. The lake would disappear. Fortunately, I had no way of looking into the future as I sat beside this beautiful little lake on that day in spring. The cataclysm that would destroy it was but a few years away.

Looking about, I noticed a great many short, dry logs perhaps six or eight inches in diameter. Gradually an idea began forming in my mind; why not build a log raft and paddle out to the little island? Putting the idea into action, I collected about a dozen logs and dragged them down the bank and into the water. Additional logs were then placed across those already in the lake. According to my plans, the logs would remain together, held in place by my weight upon the upper layer of logs. This seemed logical. Next, I found a long pole with which

Deep snow on the mountains often breaks loose and thunders down the steep slopes. One of these snow avalanches completely dammed the Madison River.

I hoped to push my raft across the lake to the island.

Gingerly I crawled onto my makeshift raft and pushed away from the steeply sloping bank. All seemed well; the logs remained in place and I floated like a swan upon the quiet surface. Looking down into the clear water I could see all sorts of aquatic insects—water boatmen and backswimmers. A few snails moved slowly across the sandy bottom. At this point a large dragonfly sailed down and alighted on one of the logs of my raft. It posed quietly in the sun, its cellophane-like wings reflecting the sunlight. The temptation was too great and I reached out and attempted to seize the insect. This was a grave error. My sudden movements caused one of the logs to float away. However, I was not worried, since enough dry logs remained to keep me afloat, and I poled on toward the island. All went well for a time and I calmly surveyed my surroundings, still intrigued by the aquatic life below the slowly moving raft.

Unobserved by me as I watched the scene unfolding below, a couple more logs seemed to develop ideas of their own and deserted me. At best, of course, this raft had been an unstable affair, but in my inexperience I had assumed that it would hold together on the quiet lake. Alas, such was not the case, as I suddenly discovered when all the logs came apart and I found myself floundering about in the deep, cold water, not a single one of the logs remaining within reach.

Self-preservation is almost automatic, as I at once discovered. I began swimming dog-fashion, flailing my arms and legs in the water. Unfortunately, in that cold climate, I had never learned to swim, but now I swam as if my life depended on it—which it did, since about a hundred feet still separated me from the island and the water was too deep for wading. I was very frightened as I struck out for the island, realizing that if I were to survive it would have to be by my own efforts.

By dint of splashing and dog-paddling, I finally reached the island, where I lay on the mossy earth to recover my breath. I looked about, taking stock of my situation. It was a very attractive bit of land, rising only a foot or so above the water, and it was bare of vegetation except for a few huckleberry bushes about a foot high. I looked across the water to where my horse was tied to a pine. He looked back at me. About fifty feet away, several of the logs from my raft floated quietly on the still surface. I looked longingly at them.

By now it was late afternoon and I realized that not a soul had any idea where I was. It was my habit to roam far and wide, never telling anyone where I was going because I never knew. And so I sat down, contemplating my situation as the sun slowly dropped down behind the western mountains. Certainly, I had no intention of spending the night here. Understandably, I was a frightened boy.

I walked around the tiny island, feeling a little like Robinson Crusoe, but the water seemed too deep for wading on all sides. I would be forced to swim, no doubt about it. Well, I had done it once; perhaps I could do it again. I realized by then that the evening chill was coming down from the high mountains. My clothing was thoroughly wet and I was cold.

From my vantage point out on the island I could look up and see the craggy peaks of the mountains, now tipped with red by the last rays of the setting sun. The surrounding forest was becoming darker and I could barely make out the form of my horse. There was nothing to do but try to swim out to one of the floating logs and perhaps use it as a buoy to paddle ashore.

Taking a deep breath, I finally entered the cold water and struck out, splashing along. However, this time, with my previous experience, it was easier and I soon reached one of the floating logs which bobbed about as I grabbed hold of it. From then on it was fairly simple; all I had to do was paddle along with one hand and kick my legs. My course was very erratic, but at last I reached the shore near where my horse was tied. He looked down at me and cocked his ears forward. Somehow I believed that he was glad that I had made it. Anyway, I certainly was.

Cold and shivering, I untied the horse, swung aboard and started back through the forest. I let the horse have his head; I figured he knew the way home better than I.

It was completely dark by the time I rode down the trail above the ranch where the lighted windows looked very welcome. I rode on down to the barn, unsaddled my horse and gave him some hay. I had no intention of telling my parents about my experience and so I went directly to my cabin in the aspen grove.

Quickly I changed into dry clothing and walked over to the house. My parents, sister, and a couple of hired men were already eating supper as I sat down at the table. There were no questions regarding my whereabouts, and I volunteered no information. What trails I walked or rode were my own private affairs; the surrounding mountains were mine to explore, and they assumed that I could take care of myself. For awhile at the lake up on Dead Man Gulch I had not been so sure, but it was there that I had learned to swim—the hard way.

I had seen an advertisement in a magazine about a man in California who, he said, was in the market for rare butterflies. Naturally I was interested. However, there was a catch; in order to sell him these rare butterflies one had to purchase his book on their identification. Nevertheless, I bought one of his books and studied it very carefully. Although I did not recognize any of the butterflies in his book, I decided to try and find some of them.

I have not previously said much about my faithful horse, Snoozer. He had been named thus because of his habit of going to sleep while standing up, and nearly falling down. He never actually fell down, always regaining his equilibrium in time. He was, however, a smart horse. Whenever I saddled him and attempted to tighten the cinch he would swell up with air. Later it would be noticed that the cinch hung loosely below his belly. He had another trick that, I assumed, was aimed at disturbing me. When going down a trail he would watch for sagebrushes that leaned in such a way as to reflect the sun. Whenever such a bush was spotted he would shy away, suddenly jumping side-wise and causing me to lose my balance and fall off. Then, having accomplished his purpose, he would stand quietly, al-lowing me to remount. Usually this sequence of events would be repeated several times a mile. I am not a horse psychologist and so do not know how he received any satisfaction from this. Eventually, however, I learned how to outwit him; whenever I spotted a shiny sagebrush I would beat him to the draw by jumping off. This was no doubt quite frustrating to his ego. In any case, old Snoozer and I understood each other and I loved him dearly. The truth was that he put up with some unusual habits of my own. Frequently I collected butterflies while rid-ing along a trail and he seemed never to be disturbed when I swung my butterfly net at some choice specimen that fluttered by.

After receiving the booklet on rare butterflies from the man in California, old Snoozer and I hit the trail. We roamed the surrounding canyons and mountains in quest of valuable specimens. One afternoon we went up Cascade Creek and then crossed over onto a high plateau, or bench, above it. The spring sun was warm and I was half asleep in the saddle. For a change, old Snoozer failed to spot any shiny sagebrushes and so I was free to daydream about the thousands of dollars I was going to make from the sale of rare butterflies.

Far away on the slopes of the distant Madison Range I spotted the forms of a number of elk feeding on a barren slope. High in the sky floated cottony clouds, their shadows slowly moving across the landscape. Near the dim trail we followed were many great boulders and upon most of them lay indolent

Part of my first butterfly and moth collection. This case took first prize at the county fair. It was the only insect collection entered.

marmots, watchful but unafraid. Earlier in the day they had probably filled their bellies with succulent plants and now were digesting them while basking in the warm sun.

Eventually, we came to an open, grassy meadow surrounded by tall sagebrush. There were many flowers and I could see lots of butterflies flitting from one to another. I dismounted and untied my butterfly net from the saddle. I had collected several specimens, all common kinds, when I noticed some mouse-gray specimens and easily scooped one up in the net. Only a quick examination of the specimen was needed for me to realize that it was one of the "rare" butterflies pictured in my new book. I remembered, too, that the price quoted was fifty cents each. Quickly I looked about and saw many more of the same kind.

In feverish excitement I began capturing more specimens and placing them in my cyanide killing jar. I was convinced that I had, indeed, found the pot of gold at the end of the rainbow. When the killing jar was full, I mounted old Snoozer and hurried home, kicking my heels against his ribs to speed him up.

Back in my cabin I got out the book and was elated to see that my specimens were actually the kind I had suspected. The book identified them as *Coenonympha haydeni*. I carefully placed them in envelopes, folded according to the directions given, and on the flap of each one I recorded the name, the date, and location of capture. The next day I mailed my collection to the dealer in California.

A couple of weeks passed and I had about given up my dreams of affluence when I received a check for the butterflies. Naturally, I was pleased. However, the man stated that the world market for this particular species was now glutted and to send no more. This was disappointing, since I knew that there were lots more of the butterflies up on the bench. In fact, the supply was almost unlimited. Thus ended my career as a collector of rare and valuable butterflies. However, I did not lose my interest in specimen collecting, since this region seemed to be particularly rich in unusual species. For example, I found, upon the high windswept ridges, many large white butterflies that I was able to identify as species of *Parnassius*. They measured about two inches across and had bright red spots on their wings. My books stated that their larvae or caterpillars fed upon various kinds of sedums and saxifrages and that related species occurred in the Alps.

Shortly after this, on a collecting trip near a beautiful stream known as Papoose Creek I found a number of butterflies that I could not find pictured in any of my books. I had been told that the foremost authority on these insects was Dr. J. H. McDunnough in Canada, and so I decided to send some of these butterflies to him. He was very kind, telling me that my butterflies were, indeed, a species new to science and that he was taking the "liberty" of naming it after me. I was tremendously thrilled and now believed that I was a real scientist. The butterfly had been named *Euphydryas hutchinsi*.

My wife, Annie Laurie, and I on the crest of the Madison Range back of the ranch. This picture was made on July 4, many years after I lived there. We had climbed from 6,000 feet at the ranch to the top of the range, elevation 10,000 feet.

By this time it was midsummer. The days were warm but the mountain nights, as always, were cold. Often there was frost in the mornings. When visitors from the East sometimes asked us what we did in the summer, our usual reply was that we had a ballgame that day!

The altitude at the ranch is nearly 6,000 feet and, as a result, many crops such as corn and tomatoes cannot be grown there. For hay we grew timothy and clover instead of alfalfa, which was the usual hay crop lower down the valley.

Even though the calendar said it was summer, large snow-banks still persisted along some of the higher ridges. Some of these snowbanks would last until August, only a short time before snow began to fall again. On a few of the higher mountains these snow accumulations never do melt and thus become glaciers. Glaciers occur on many Montana mountains, probably the most unusual of which is Grasshopper Glacier, located in

Grasshopper Glacier, located at 11,000 feet in the Beartooth Moun-tains. The dark bands in the glacier are grasshoppers, frozen in the ice for over five hundred years.

the Beartooth Range just north of Yellowstone Park. Its elevation is about 11,000 feet and can only be reached by a trail. Some of the surrounding peaks rise to 13,000 feet and the scenery is beautiful and spectacular. This glacier is about fifty feet thick at its lower end and perhaps a mile in width. Just below it is a lake into which the water from the melting glacier flows. Many years ago it was discovered that millions of grasshoppers (Rocky Mountain locusts) were imbedded in the glacial ice and perfectly preserved. Carbon-14 dating techniques showed that these grasshoppers were about five hundred years old. Periodically the face of the glacier melts, dropping large numbers of the insects into the lake where they are fed upon by fish. It is believed that large migrating swarms of grasshoppers once passed over the mountains where, cooled by rising air currents, they settled upon the ice and were frozen. Later, snows covered the layers of grasshoppers and preserved them.

My first knowledge of this remarkable glacier occurred one day in midsummer when two professors from Montana State University stopped by the ranch. Finding that I was interested in insects and being shown my collections, they told me that they had just returned from a trip to Grasshopper Glacier. They also showed me some of the preserved specimens. This was my first actual contact with professional entomologists and I was very much impressed.

Upon their return to the university they sent me additional equipment to help me with my work. Up until this time I had never realized that such a fascinating subject could actually become a full-time career. The professors' names were R. A. Cooley and J. R. Parker. Later, when I entered the university, they became my professors and remained my close friends until their deaths many years later.

4
YELLOWSTONE BY COVERED WAGON

YELLOWSTONE NATIONAL PARK is probably the most remarkable natural region in North America. Millions of years ago a vast intrusion of molten magma pushed out of the earth's interior and into the area beneath what is now the park. Heat from this vast pool of hot magma is what gives rise to the numerous hot springs and geysers found there. Probably the first white man to view the wonders of the region was John Colter, who was captured there in 1808 by the local Indians and barely escaped with his life. He eventually told about the wonders he had seen, and the area became known as Colter's Hell because of the boiling pools and spouting geysers. It became the first National Park, established in 1872.

The summer that we made our trip through Yellowstone Park by covered wagon was one I remember vividly and with pleasure. Automobiles were not admitted into the park until later (1915). Tourists without their own saddle horses or wagons were taken through the park by horse-drawn stagecoaches, patterned after the old Western coaches. They had no springs. Instead, the bodies were suspended on heavy leather straps, or bands, extending from front to back. As a result, the "dudes"

When Grotto Geyser in Yellowstone National Park erupts, the boiling water emerges from several vents.

riding therein experienced continuous rocking motions like ships at sea. These coaches picked up passengers at West Yellowstone and carried them through the park. Often there would be a dozen or more coaches in a group, and the passengers spent the nights at the large hotels located at Old Faithful, Yellowstone Lake, and the Grand Canyon.

It was during this particular summer that a real old-time stagecoach robbery occurred, when one of these strings of coaches was near Dunraven Pass. A group of armed and masked men stopped the lead coach and forced all the passengers to dismount, after which their valuables were taken. Back at the rear of the line of coaches was a lady from the East who did not want to miss out on the "fun" and so forced the driver to pull on up to where the action was. She wanted to be able to tell her friends in the East that she had actually been in an old-time stagecoach robbery, probably the last to take place in the West. I have often wondered what the other passengers in that particular coach had to say to her after their valuables had been removed. The highwaymen were never apprehended.

The preparations for our covered-wagon trip were extensive. A covered wagon was available, but all the necessary provisions had to be obtained and packed, since there would be no grocery stores along the way. We would sleep in a tent.

Accompanying my father, mother, sister, and me would be a cousin from the East, named Best, and my aunt Vi (Viola). This aunt was something of a character, as will become evident. Cousin Best and Aunt Vi would ride on horseback while the rest of us rode in the wagon.

On a clear July day we took off up the road to West Yellowstone, camping the first night at a beautiful spot along the Madison River. All went well at this shakedown camp and the next day we arrived at West Yellowstone, the western entrance to the park.

At this time there was no National Park Service, the park being run by the U.S. Army. The National Park Service was not established until 1916. While in the Park we would be required to register at a Soldier Station every few miles.

We drove up to the Park entrance and registered. The soldier on duty asked if we had any "firearms or firewater." When assured that we had neither, we were allowed to drive on in. Cousin Best rode along with us on his horse, but Aunt Vi decided at the last minute to look the town over and then catch up with us wherever we camped inside the park.

A couple of miles beyond the entrance we came to a pretty meadow beside the Madison River and decided to camp. The team was unhitched and hobbled to prevent their wandering away too far during the night. The tent was then put up and the beds made. Vi had not yet shown up, so we cooked supper over a campfire and ate. I went out along the riverbank to look at the flowers and plants, but these seemed no different, of course, from those around the home ranch. There were, however, several insects I had not previously seen.

By this time it was almost dark and Vi had not yet appeared, causing considerable concern about her whereabouts. At last my father decided to saddle a horse and ride back to West Yellowstone to locate her if possible. After he left we sat around the fire talking, often looking fearfully into the surrounding timber in case a grizzly bear should approach. We had been warned to look out for them. None appeared, however, and eventually my sister and I went to bed.

Not long after this my father and Aunt Vi arrived. After considerable searching he had finally located her at a local dance to which she had unerringly been attracted. She was warned never to wander off again. She didn't; at least not on this trip, after discovering that there really were many bears and that they could be dangerous, especially the grizzlies.

The next morning my father and Cousin Best went looking for the horses, which had wandered off about a mile, even though the hobbles were supposed to prevent their doing so.

The second night was more or less a repetition of the first, except that at this camp a soldier came down and sat for awhile at our campfire. After a time he asked if we needed any coffee. When told that we could use a little, he left, returning with a fifty-pound bag of unground coffee. He sold the coffee to us at a ridiculous price and this supply lasted us all the rest of the summer. Many years later, when I was older and wiser, I realized that the coffee had come from GI stores, the soldier's means of obtaining a little extra spending money.

The next night we camped near Fountain Paint Pots. This was our first contact with one of the hot geyser areas of the region and I was much impressed. In addition to several boiling pools, there were the Paint Pots, bubbling pools of pastel-

YELLOWSTONE BY COVERED WAGON

colored mud. The strange thing to me was that the various colors did not seem to mix, even though they were adjacent to each other.

At that time there were few rules or restrictions and so I was free to collect "specimens." Surrounding most of the geysers and boiling pools were numerous colorful encrustations of geyserite and other minerals which attracted my interest, and I began accumulating examples to take home. Soon I had a huge pile of these specimens in the back of the wagon, causing my father to warn me that these things were heavy and if my activities continued there would eventually be nowhere for anyone to ride. I tried, but each time I saw a pretty mineral specimen I could not resist temptation and before the end of the trip I had to start throwing my treasured specimens away. However, I always seemed to find more.

It was not until years later that I learned that the beautiful coloration of the geysers and hot springs was due to the presence of blue-green algae, living plants that had adapted to life in the hot water. At the time I did notice that where the water first flowed out of the ground the colors were different from those in the cooler water after it had flowed some distance in the open. This, I now know, was because different species of algae thrive in waters of different temperatures. Most characteristic of all these geyser areas, I noticed, was their rotten-egg odor, caused, I was told, by the presence of sulphur.

Moose and elk were abundant along the road, showing far less fear than in later years after automobiles had been allowed in the Park. Moose, feeding along the margins of the rivers, lifted their great antlered heads to gaze momentarily at us, then went on feeding beneath the water. Wild geese were everywhere. I could see the mothers and their young swimming along in the water, oblivious to our passing. One night several elk bedded down near our camp and, early in the morning, we heard their trumpeting calls. It was difficult for me to believe that these sounds had been made by such large animals.

We reached Old Faithful geyser without incident a day or so later. I had heard tales of this natural phenomenon, but was unprepared for the display. We arrived there late in the evening, after the sun had dropped down behind the mountains and it was very cold. The elevation was several thousand feet higher than that at the ranch and so night temperatures were considerably lower, often reaching the freezing point at this time of the year.

There were several people standing around waiting for Old Faithful to play and we joined them. They said it was amost time. My natural curiosity getting the better of me, I went up and looked down into the opening from which the hot water would gush. It didn't look very impressive; it was merely a small hole in the top of a high mound.

Shortly, there was a low gurgling sound beneath my feet and then a small jet of water rushed out of the opening. It rose to only about ten feet. I was disappointed, but continued to watch.

After a few more seconds, the real show got underway; a powerful fountain of hot water and steam shot seventy-five feet into the air, forcing me to beat a hasty retreat to avoid being scalded by the hot water falling all around me. It was an awe-inspiring show and I was then impressed.

Many years later I was present when a most amusing incident occurred during one of the periodic eruptions of Old Faithful. Two young men had obtained an old automobile steering wheel and jammed its axle into the ground a short distance from the famous geyser. As usual, a Park Ranger had arrived to lecture the tourists about it and he had taken his place in front of the crowd, which watched with interest the prespouting activity of the geyser. One of the young men had stationed himself near the Ranger.

When the time was about right for the main display, the man

Old Faithful geyser, probably the world's most famous geyser. Boiling water gushes 75 feet or more into the air at approximately 65-minute intervals. It has been known to reach 250 feet.

near the Ranger yelled, "Let her go, Bill." At this, Bill spun the
wheel and Old Faithful, living up to her reputation for punctu-
ality, erupted into the air with a loud noise. Naturally, this
caused considerable mirth in the crowd, perhaps embarrassing
the nonplused Ranger. However, Park Rangers do have senses
of humor, as I later learned on many occasions in several National Parks.

The next morning we left Old Faithful and, that night, arrived at Yellowstone Lake where we found a desirable spot to
camp near the shore and there set up our tent. As usual, our
horses were hobbled and turned loose to graze on the lush
grass. Perhaps it should be explained to the uninitiated that
horse hobbles consist of two straps having buckles which are
placed around a horse's front feet. These straps are connected
to each other by several links of chain. When hobbled, a horse
can walk slowly about and graze, but it usually cannot wander

*Along the roadside near Yellowstone Lake we saw buffalo grazing
peacefully. Two elk are in the background.*

very far away from camp. However, we did have one horse that could cover a lot of territory during the night in spite of the hindrance imposed by the hobbles. A prime example of this occurred at the lake camp.

The next morning when my father went looking for the horses, they were all located within half a mile. All, that is, except Old Dan, named after Dan Patch. Though my father searched half the morning, Old Dan could not be found and so when a soldier rode by his aid was requested.

About noon the soldier returned, leading Old Dan. He had traveled more than two miles during the night, probably frightened by a bear. Certainly Old Dan had good reason to fear bears, since he bore a long scar on his rump resulting from an encounter with a grizzly near the ranch years before.

Having found all our horses, we harnessed up and took off from the West Thumb of the lake, following along the shore. This was the largest body of water I had ever seen and I was amazed that I could not even see across it. Actually, it is the second largest lake in the world at that altitude. The largest is Lake Titicaca on the Peru-Bolivia boundary at 12,500 feet elevation. Yellowstone Lake is at 7,731 feet and has an area of 139 square miles.

At the edge of the lake, at one place, there was a small hot pool and it was a common practice at the time for fishermen to hook trout in the lake and then drop them, still on the line, into the hot pool to cook. It was a very convenient arrangement but, in later years, the practice was stopped, being considered cruel.

As we drove leisurely along the road near the lake we saw many deer and elk and, in one place, a group of sandhill cranes feeding in a marshy area. All the wildlife was very tame and paid little attention to us. Once we came upon several buffalo grazing quietly near the road.

Those who now travel down the congested highways of Yellowstone Park can have no conception of the pleasant and

Mud Geyser. Hot, boiling mud gushes periodically out of an opening at the back. It is an awesome sight.

leisurely travel afforded by a covered-wagon journey such as ours. Of necessity, there can be no hurry. Often I left the wagon and walked along, looking at things beside the road. When tired, I climbed aboard again to rest and watch the passing scene.

Eventually we left the lake and followed along the Yellowstone River, after a few hours coming to the famous Mud Volcano, then called Mud Geyser. As we approached we saw about a dozen of the yellow Park stagecoaches stopped beside the road and the passengers walking about, most of them looking at the geyser.

This Mud Geyser was, to me, rather gruesome. From a large cavity in the mountainside there periodically gushed great floods of boiling mud and escaping steam, accompanied by loud sound effects. The hot mud gushed out and then receded at regular intervals, and there was little doubt in my mind that tremendous heat lay not far beneath the mountain. One of the tourists standing in awe a short distance away, remarked, "Hell is not far from this place." I agreed with him.

We camped that night along the Yellowstone River in a pretty meadow surrounded by sagebrush. Here the grass was lush and so the horses were picketed instead of being hobbled. My father believed that the horses could graze sufficiently within the circle afforded by the lengths of picket ropes and, thus, could not wander away as they often did.

We struck our tent and got underway very early the following morning, starting across the wide Hayden Valley. Sometimes the road crossed over broad, sagebrush-covered benches, then dropped down near the wide Yellowstone River.

I had never seen such a river. It flowed gently between grassy banks and I could see that its bottom was covered with long aquatic plants that waved gently in the current. Most interesting were the water birds that were present in astonishing variety and numbers. Trumpeter swans rode gracefully upon the surface, their white forms mirrored in the water. Canada geese were everywhere. Some had little groups of goslings paddling alongside. Even from a distance we could hear the mixed voices of the large water birds, honking and squawking. This, I thought, was the way it was before the first white men came to this wild place.

We stopped for the noon meal not far from the river and, while the food was being prepared, I walked some distance away through the tall sagebrush to see what I could find at a bend of the river, now hidden from view. Arriving at a small bluff, I lay down on my belly and peeked over the edge and down to the river. To my surprise, there was a large bull moose feeding in the water some distance from the shore. It had enormous antlers and would submerge almost its entire head

A bull moose feeds on aquatic plants in the shallow Yellowstone River in Hayden Valley.

each time it lowered it to feed upon the underwater plants. I had once been told that a moose can hold its breath for only about one and a half minutes when browsing under water, and this one seemed to follow this rule. Each time it raised its great head, it looked around, then went on feeding again. Apparently it did not see me. At least it gave no indication that it did.

A short distance upstream from the moose was a tiny, willow-covered island and suddenly I spotted a pair of beavers resting in some tall grass at one end. They, like the moose, were completely oblivious to my presence, and I saw that they were busily scratching lice as they sat in the warm summer sun. I had read that beavers are infested with a beetle parasite, a most unusual habit for a beetle, and assumed this was what was causing them to scratch.

I crouched in the tall sagebrush for a long while, watching the moose and the beavers. Soon a great blue heron came into view, walking sedately along the bank. At this point I heard a loud call and knew that dinner was ready, and so was forced to abandon my interesting observations.

After dinner the horses were hitched up again and we continued our slow progress down the dusty road across the sagebrush-covered hills of Hayden Valley. Once we saw a lone coyote skulking through the tall grass. As we approached the end of the valley, it narrowed down and the timbered slopes of the mountains came near the road.

By this time it was almost dusk and when we looked toward the left we saw a large herd of elk filing down the mountainside toward the river. It was a beautiful sight and one that I was to remember the rest of my life. Many of the elk were bulls adorned with great, spreading antlers held high and proud. The herd crossed the road ahead of us, not even looking in our direction. They ambled down near the river and milled about, some of them drinking from a quiet pool. To me it was a wild and primitive scene, the way it once was and the way it should be preserved forever. I watched entranced at this close-up view of the elk engaging in their daily migration down out of the mountains to graze and to drink from the mirror-like waters of the wide river.

Leaving Hayden Valley, we eventually arrived at a point near the Grand Canyon and camped beside the road. It was an attractive spot, not far from the river, but we were pestered by

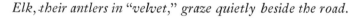
Elk, their antlers in "velvet," graze quietly beside the road.

bears—grizzlies, blacks, and browns. It was not difficult to chase the blacks and browns away, but the grizzlies were more of a problem. They paid little attention to our rock-throwing or noise. Probably they had been attracted by the smell of cooking food. We were getting desperate when an armed soldier came by and fired his rifle into the air a couple of times, causing them to run off, and we saw them no more. I noted with interest that the blacks and browns seemed afraid of the grizzlies and would not go near them. Certainly they were, and are, vicious beasts that had best be left alone.

Due to the close proximity of the bears at this camp site, the horses were picketed near the camp and we retired with considerable misgivings. It was feared that the bears might return and plunder our food supplies. However, the night passed quietly and the next morning it was very cold with gray mist hanging over the river. However, warmed by a roaring fire, we cooked breakfast and then continued on down the road. Soon we could hear the sound of the great waterfall, and eventually came to the viewing place known as Inspiration Point where we looked down into the vast canyon and saw the Yellowstone River plunging down 308 feet into a misty caldron of seething water. It was, and still is, an awe-inspiring sight, and one that once seen is never forgotten. The canyon itself is nearly a mile wide and a mile deep, its walls stained yellow, red, and orange by minerals from hot springs. Far down I could see jets of steam issuing from small vents, and here and there on crags were perched the nests of eagles. Now and again the eagles sailed out across the vast chasm, their forms almost lost in the immensity of the space spread out far below. It is one of the world's most spectacular views and I turned away, awed and a little frightened by the spectacle.

I have stood at Inspiration Point many times since then, but have never lost the feeling of my own insignificance in the face of that vast cavity, slashed out of the earth by the tumbling

Yellowstone River plunges 308 feet to the bottom of the Grand Canyon of the Yellowstone. It was, and is, an awe-inspiring sight.

waters of the river, acting slowly over millions of years. It is a sight that one remembers with reverence for the great forces that formed the earth.

Nothing unusual occurred along that portion of our covered-wagon trip. Each night was a repetition of previous ones; the horses often strayed away during the night and had to be searched for. We had by now settled into a routine. We struggled up over Dunraven Pass, reaching an elevation of nearly 9,000 feet. The road over the pass was very rocky and narrow but it was negotiated without difficulty. However, the horses had to be given rest periods several times on the way up. During one of these rest periods a large Rocky Mountain bighorn ram was spotted on a distant bluff, his form etched darkly against the sky. Still as a statue, his great coiled horns looked as if they had been carved from ivory.

The mountainside was covered with low-growing vegetation, well adapted to the rigorous climate at that elevation. Walking around near the road, I noticed a number of small blue flowers and, upon picking one, discovered that it smelled exactly like a skunk. Later, back at the ranch, I looked up the flower in one of my books and found it to be a member of the Phlox family known appropriately as skunkflower (*Polemonium viscosum*). Also upon the mountainside were many low-growing sedums and lichens, common and characteristic plants of the high, wind-swept Rockies where the climate is essentially arctic in nature.

We dropped down from Dunraven Pass and continued on our way. Game animals were abundant everywhere. We came eventually to Mammoth Hot Springs, but after all the other hot springs and geysers I was not especially impressed. Here, too, we encountered a long string of stagecoaches with many "dudes," as we called them, taking in the sights. We camped near the hot springs.

Leaving Mammoth Hot Springs, the road meandered south toward Norris Geyser Basin. At one place, beside the road, we came to Appollinaris Spring and we all got out and took a drink of the water from our tin cups. I didn't like it; it tasted like alum and one small sip was all I cared for.

The remainder of our covered-wagon trip was uneventful and we arrived back at the home ranch with much to talk about. I unloaded my mineral specimens and placed them on a special shelf in my cottage where I kept them for a long while. However, as is the usual course of events with such things, I gradually lost interest in them and they were discarded.

Now, looking back upon that covered-wagon trip, I realize just how privileged I was to have experienced it. With this type of travel there was time to see at close range the wonders of Nature. There were, of course, inconveniences, but, to me, the virtues of the slow travel outweighed the difficulties. Certainly there was no energy problem; the "fuel" grew along the way.

5

NIGHT OF THE
TREMBLING MOUNTAINS

ONE CANNOT live in the Rockies without becoming aware of past geological activity, of the great cataclysmic events that shaped them. However, we are usually lulled into complacency, assuming that these events belong to the distant past and will never occur again. Many times while climbing in the mountains I noticed outcroppings of ancient lava flows and stratas that had been bent and twisted. The Madison Range back of the ranch thrusts up to nearly 10,000 feet and its crest is covered with masses of shalelike stone. A close examination of this stone reveals large numbers of fossilized crinoids, primitive animals that once lived in the sea. Yet here are their remains, preserved in stone, and lifted nearly two miles above the sea where they lived many millions of years ago. This is concrete evidence of the vast uplifting processes that formed the range. It is not difficult, of course, to find numerous other evidences of change.

In my periodical expeditions into the mountains near the ranch I saw many results of past volcanic changes, but I knew little geology and so could not interpret the things I saw. The mountains seemed quiet and solid, and I did not realize that, deep within the earth below, powerful tensions were even then

The earthquake of 1959 caused great cracks in the mountainside near the ranch.

building up. I realize now that these great mountain masses, whose crests reached far into the skies, were merely waiting, marking time so to speak, between periods of violence and change.

Extending along the base of the range back of the ranch there was a definite break in the slope. I often pondered over this, wondering what had caused it. Someone once told me that it was the shoreline of an ancient lake. Certainly this was what it appeared to be, and in my lack of geological knowledge, I never questioned it.

I now realize that this was a fault line, a point where the underlying stony structure of the mountains had once moved, one portion shifting with reference to the other. When such an event occurs, the result is an earthquake. There were actually several of these faults in the vicinity of the ranch, as later events were to prove so dramatically. Probably we at the ranch should have realized that we were practically sitting on top of one of these faults, since mild earthquakes were a common occurrence as far back as I can remember. Dishes were often shaken off shelves and large boulders frequently thundered down from the mountainside above the house. Once a boulder as large as a small cottage rolled down, stopping only ten feet short of crashing through the ranch house. Still, we were not perturbed. One tends to assume that mountains are eternal and will always remain as they are. We were eventually to discover that such is not the case. One night the great tensions building up within the mountains reached the breaking point and they shook themselves like a dog emerging from the water.

The events I am about to describe began at 11:37 P.M. on August 17, 1959, a number of years after I had left Montana to pursue a career as a professional biologist.

Unfortunately, I was unable to return until things had settled down. But when I did return several months later I found many changes. The great cliffs above the ranch where I had often watched cliff swallows in their nesting had been greatly altered. Even the contours of the surrounding mountains looked so different that I hardly recognized them at all.

Things at the ranch on this fateful night had been about normal. There were several guests and everyone had retired. Then, near midnight, there came a vigorous shaking and trembling of the earth, accompanied by loud rumbling sounds. The mountains appeared to be shaking to their very foundations. Everyone, of course, rushed outside, but nothing could be seen in the darkness. However, it was obvious that great boulders from the cliffs above the ranch house were thundering down toward the level ground. The ground itself was moving, as if in the grip of a giant hand. From the distant mountains came roaring and thundering sounds as the earth shuddered and vibrated. The waiting mountains had reached a climax. Deep below them, enormous tensions had been building up for centuries and these tensions were suddenly released, creating

These are the cliffs above the ranch where I often climbed up to watch cliff swallows building their nests. (See next photograph.)

After the earthquake. Notice how my swallow cliffs were tumbled down. Some boulders as large as houses rolled down near the ranch.

shock waves that spread away from the epicenters, or points of origin.

The heaving and trembling of the mountains settled down to some extent after a time, but intermittent aftershocks continued. Naturally, no one slept the remainder of the night and, when dawn came at last, it was seen that the bed of the river below the ranch house was dry. Everything in the house was in a shambles.

The people at the ranch realized by this time that a major earthquake had occurred, but most types of communication were ineffective or badly garbled. Unknown to those at the ranch, a major tragedy had occurred near the mouth of the Madison Canyon, only about five miles upriver. At this point, just before the Madison River emerges from the Madison Range, a great landslide had dammed up the river and buried twenty-nine people beneath several hundred feet of earth and

The Madison River flows out of the Madison Range at this point. During the great 1959 earthquake the side of the mountain at the right slid down and completely blocked the river.

Only a year before the 1959 earthquake, my family enjoyed a picnic at the attractive site now buried beneath more than 300 feet of stone and earth.

stone. This, of course, accounted for the fact that the river had ceased flowing past the ranch.

The point where this tragedy occurred was about six miles below a large storage reservoir, Hebgen Dam. This reservoir is more than seven miles long and, in some places, nearly a mile wide. It was constructed as a storage site to control the flow of water to Madison Dam, located about fifty miles below, where power is generated to serve most of the area.

The great slide had happened at the attractive Rock Creek campground, a favored site for trailer and tent campers and where many people had been camped on the night of the disaster. As the story was eventually pieced together by survivors, here is the sequence of events: the campers were awakened by the swaying and shaking of the trees and the trembling of the earth. Shortly, they saw a huge wave of water come rushing down the canyon. The next instant the entire side of the mountain on the opposite side of the canyon, half a mile wide and

1,300 feet high, suddenly tore loose and about 85 million cubic yards of earth and stone rushed down into and across the river, burying the campers beneath the debris. These people are still there. The survivors later told harrowing tales of personal fear and narrow escapes. To them, the world seemed to be coming to its end in a night of sheer terror.

One of the first effects of the quake had been the tilting of Hebgen Lake. This caused a tidal wave nearly twenty feet high to rush down and spill over the concrete dam and on down the canyon. A few minutes later the great slide broke loose and thundered across the river, burying everything in its path, including many of the campers.

By strange coincidence, this event occurred at about the same point in Madison Canyon as had the great snowslide so many years before, and which had also dammed the river.

The dam formed by the earthquake completely blocked the large stream. It was nearly five hundred feet high and, of course, the waters of the Madison River began backing up above it. It was soon evident that the river would eventually begin flowing over the dam and, if this dam should not hold, the accumulated water would then rush down the valley, destroying towns and ranches along the way. Great alarm was felt at Ennis, about forty-five miles downriver. It was decided to evacuate the town during the early morning hours.

At this time, reports from the disaster area were garbled and just what had occurred was not known. During this period nothing of concrete nature was known concerning the quake or its local results. We had relatives living at Ennis and they feared that the entire Hutchins family at the ranch had been wiped out. As a result, an aunt had to be rushed to a hospital suffering from a nervous breakdown.

Meanwhile, up at the ranch, located close to the epicenter of the earthquake, the situation looked grave. They, too, considered seriously the possibility that the dam created by the quake might break and release a great flood of water. If this were to actually occur, all the buildings would certainly be washed away.

Within a few hours, a situation of major catastrophe was declared and heavy earth-moving equipment was requisitioned from all points in the Northwest. The equipment began arriving at the slide within a few days, and a spillway paved with stone was quickly constructed. This, it was hoped, would prevent the water from cutting away the fresh earth when it began flowing over the top of the dam.

In the meantime, the water continued to rise behind the dam, gradually filling up the new lake. Those living downriver continued to worry. My relatives at the ranch—the closest one to the quake—moved into a house trailer located up on a bench, about a hundred feet above the level of the river. They remained there all the rest of the summer—just in case.

Several weeks were required for the dammed water to begin flowing over the man-made spillway. This, indeed, was a crucial period and everyone waited to see what would happen. Fortunately, the dam held. The impounded water began flowing over the spillway and down the dry river bed.

Tourists who visit the area now may see and marvel at the large lake that was suddenly created by one of Nature's mighty cataclysms. On road maps it is designated as Quake Lake, and it will be there forever—or perhaps until the mountains tremble again.

I visited the home ranch several months after the earthquake and was astonished at the changes in the vicinity. Up at Dead Man Gulch an enormous mass of stone and earth had slipped down the mountain. Strangely, the largest slide had moved down as a single mass and a small forest upon it was almost undisturbed. The little lake where I had learned to swim was gone, covered by debris.

Down at the ranch there were numerous changes. The spring

Above: *This view, taken downstream, shows the vast slide that dammed the river. A new lake is already forming above it (foreground).*

Right: *My nephew inspects cracks in the earth after the earthquake. This is the pasture where I once kept my saddle horse.*

A road beside Hebgen Dam, just above the great slide, was destroyed by the earthquake.

where I had once collected aquatic insects was dry. Nearby, in the pasture where I had once kept old Snoozer, there were now large cracks in the ground.

At the home ranch were several elk and deer heads hanging from the walls. Since the ceiling was low, the tips of the antlers were but a few inches below it. I was intrigued by the fact that these antlers had "hooked" the ceiling during the quake, making many indentations that were clearly visible. Evidently, the mounted heads had bounced up and down during the violent earth movements.

Several miles above our ranch I saw a place where the earth had shifted laterally about ten feet, causing a fence that crossed it to be out of line by an equal distance. Here, too, there were huge cracks in the earth. Also, the road at one point was out of line by more than twenty feet.

I now realize that the "eternal" mountains are not eternal after all. To me, they always seemed to be waiting. Now I know what they had been waiting for: one of the great periodic changes that had brought them into being. Mountains rest quietly upon the land, seemingly solid and immovable. Unknown to us, however, there are deeply hidden forces at work, building up stresses and strains that will in time reach a breaking point. When this occurs, the mountains and the land move. As one person who was present at the great earthquake put it, "The ground just got up and bucked like a horse." It was one of the six strongest earthquakes ever recorded in the United States, registering magnitude 7.1 on the Richter scale.

I now live for part of each year in the Great Smoky Mountains of Tennessee where I have experienced minor earthquakes. These great mountains are very ancient, far older than the Rockies, yet they are not completely dormant. Perhaps they will one day come to life and tremble with renewed vigor. Only time can tell. Like the Rockies, they are perhaps waiting for coming events in the continuing sequence of change.

6

THE DESERT AND THE DEEP SOUTH

IT WAS inevitable that I should eventually obtain a college degree if my ambition to become a professional biologist was to be realized. At Montana State College (now a university) I majored in entomology and zoology under Professor R. A. Cooley, one of the men who had stopped by the ranch on the way back from Grasshopper Glacier several years before. At this time Professor Cooley was involved in research on Rocky Mountain spotted fever and shortly thereafter left for South Africa in search of tick parasites, in the hope that they might be helpful in destroying the ticks that transmitted spotted fever. He was gone a year and I followed his activities with great interest. Unfortunately, he was not successful in finding effective parasites, but he did have some interesting experiences in the Dark Continent, reminiscent of Stanley's search for Livingstone. The professor's tales of the jungles fired me with a desire to go there.

Unfortunately, I was never able to realize this ambition. However, I was still interested in tropical jungles and lands when graduation approached. The United Fruit Company, at that time, offered me a position in Central America where I

The Superstition Mountains of Arizona are barren, desert mountains with characteristic vegetation. Most conspicuous of the plants is the great saguaro cactus.

would be doing research on banana insects. I was advised by my professors to do graduate work before taking off into the jungles, and so I went to Mississippi State University and enrolled, having obtained a delay from United Fruit. There, after a few months, I developed itchy feet and took off for Arizona on a temporary entomological job for the U.S. Government.

I traveled to Tempe, Arizona, where I had my first experience in a real desert area. My entomological work was not especially challenging, but I did take every opportunity to explore the surrounding deserts and mountains.

Not far from Tempe rise the famous Superstition Mountains,

barren desert mountains covered with cacti, ocotillo, and agave. It is somewhere in these mountains that lies the nebulous Lost Dutchman mine, a site, it was said, of a fabulous hoard of gold. At the time of my explorations there, it was not unusual for any lone wanderer to be shot on sight, on the bare chance that he might possess a map to the mine's location. However, I did not then know of such danger and so roamed these stark mountains oblivious to hazards.

On my first day off from my duties I hiked across the desert toward the distant mountains. Just how distant they were took me some time to realize. In the clear desert air the far-off mountains appeared much nearer than they actually were, and so I was surprised at the distance.

The sandy floor of the desert was covered with plants I had never seen, most of them cacti. Dominating the scene were the tall forms of the great saguaros, some of them more than twenty feet tall, their great arms rising grotesquely like human arms in supplication. Far up on some of them I saw small cavities excavated by woodpeckers and later used by tiny owls as nesting sites. Barrel cacti grew everywhere on the barren floor of the dreary land. Far up in the sky several buzzards circled endlessly in search of carrion.

About noon I finally reached the base of the Superstition Mountains and, after locating a dim trail, began climbing up through a dry arroyo. The going was rough but I made good progress, eventually reaching a water hole that had been scoured out by eons of rushing torrents during the infrequent rains. I sat down to eat my lunch, watching with interest several small lizards darting about among the barren rocks. They were desert night lizards (*Xantusia*).

The time was early spring and some of the desert cacti were just opening their blooms to numerous bees. I rested quietly upon a sun-warmed boulder, watching the scene. Far below my perch I could look out across the desert floor stretching far away toward the south. It was covered with thousands of saguaros interspersed with ocotillos and creosote bushes. A desert bird, whose name I did not know, sang from a tall Joshua tree, or yucca.

After a time I continued climbing on up the dry arroyo, eventually reaching the top of the mountain. Here there were many cacti and a number of century plants, or agaves, some with tall flowering stalks rising from their centers. As I walked slowly along I gradually realized that most of the desert plants were quite evenly spaced with reference to each other. Thinking the matter over, I came to the conclusion that, in this region of deficient rainfall, plants can grow only as close together as the reach of their roots. Thus, there is a definite limitation to their density of growth.

In several places along the way I noticed areas that had been rooted up by some animal. At the time I could not imagine what animal it could be. I pushed on, examining the varied cacti growing in the sandy earth. Here and there were prostrate saguaros, dead and decaying, their spiny flesh weathered away, leaving hard riblike skeletons exposed to the desert sun. These great cacti grow to great age, some perhaps reaching several hundred years old.

While examining one of these derelicts, I kicked it apart to see what it was like inside. Much to my astonishment I exposed a large reptile more than a foot in length, with mottled red and black pebbled skin. It was heavy bodied and had a swollen tail. This, I realized, was a gila monster, one of the most interesting of all the desert reptiles. They are quite poisonous, having poison glands that secrete a toxic venom. They feed upon birds' eggs and, perhaps, insects and scorpions.

The gila monster was sluggish, rendered so by the night chill of the desert, not yet heated up by the sun. I decided to take this specimen back with me, but realized that this posed some problems. How could I carry it back to my hotel?

Fortunately, I still had the cloth bag in which my lunch had been carried and I was finally able to get the large lizard inside it. It made no effort to struggle or escape, and so I carried it along, holding the bag away from my body to avoid being bitten. Later, back at my hotel, I kept the specimen hidden in a box, hoping that the maid would not see it and complain to the management that I had a deadly creature in my room. The next day I bought a dozen eggs from a grocery and broke one of them into a saucer and was pleased when the reptile lapped it up. It was a cooperative "pet," approaching the saucer to lap up the eggs like a cat lapping up milk. It was always very slow and sluggish in its actions, and so I gradually began treating it rather carelessly. One day, however, I made the error of trying to pick it up. This was a mistake. The gila monster suddenly turned around with lightning speed and attempted to bite me. I had not realized that it could move so fast. After this I treated it with greater respect.

After my return to Mississippi I kept the beast in a cage, continuing to feed it on hen eggs. Apparently its tail served as a fat storage site and, when fed regularly, its tail became quite swollen. However, one summer I was absent, delegating its feeding to a student. Upon my return in the fall, the gila monster's tail resembled that of a rat. However, within a couple of weeks, on a regular diet of eggs, its tail again became swollen with contained fat.

Back on the Superstition Mountains, I continued hiking up the gentle slope, walking now toward some barren cliffs rising above me. The sun was warmer and numerous insects were buzzing about. Nothing moved in the vast world spreading away from the desert mountains and I paused to contemplate the scene. Abruptly I became aware of something moving among some boulders ahead of me and watched, hoping to see what it was. I had about decided that my eyes had deceived me

The author at the crest of the Superstition Mountains, in a picture taken by delayed action shutter. Somewhere in these mountains lies the famous Lost Dutchman gold mine.

when three javelina hogs (collared peccaries) came into view. I had heard tales of these wild peccaries and of the danger of encountering them, and so I regarded these with some trepidation.

The hogs were gray and of very slender form like a domestic

razorback. There were several young ones in the group, having
dark stripes down their backs. At their distance from me I
couldn't tell whether or not they possessed tusks, but I took no
chance and retreated back down the mountain, leaving them to
go their own way unmolested. I now realized that these animals
were what had been rooting up the ground in several spots
along the trail I had followed up the mountains.

Slowly I meandered back down the steep side of the Superstition Mountains and then back across the level desert floor to
my car, carrying the gila monster along.

The desert, I had found, was a most fascinating place to a
biologist. It is unlike any other habitat on earth, forcing its own
severe conditions of life upon all the plants and animals that
dwell there. During my sojourn in Arizona I returned again and
again to the surrounding deserts, marveling at the manner in
which the living things had adapted themselves to the sere
habitat.

Eventually my work with the federal government came to an
end and I returned to the Deep South, to Mississippi State
University to take up graduate work again. There I met and
married the girl who was to share my life through thick and,
often, thin. Annie Laurie, also a graduate student in biological
science, has through the years been helpful and sympathetic to
all the problems I have encountered, first as a young professor
and, later, as a writer.

After a year of graduate study and the acquiring of a Mas-
ter's Degree, I informed the United Fruit Company that I was
then ready to go to Central America. They told me that this
would be fine and made reservations for me on one of their
"banana" boats to Honduras. There was a catch, however; they
said that they assumed that I was still single, since there were
no quarters for married men in the primitive area where I
would be stationed. That was that, and so ended my short career as a research entomologist for the great United Fruit
Company.

In the face of this denouement I elected to pursue further graduate studies at Iowa State University, where I was eventually awarded a Ph.D. After this I returned to the South to become a professor of entomology and zoology at Mississippi State University.

These were formative years. In addition to teaching I found time to commence writing articles for magazines and Sunday supplements, all illustrated with my own photographs. I had become rather proficient in this craft while still at Montana State University, and this experience was now a tremendous help with publishers. Since I was able to supply my own photographs, they did not need to seek them elsewhere to illustrate my articles. Writing is probably the world's most competitive profession. Many people have the desire to write, but have nothing unusual or interesting to write about. What little successes I have had in this field have been largely due to the patient help of various editors. There was also a literary agent who thought that I had some ability and so obtained a contract from a well-known publisher to write four books about plants and animals. This was a start and I got busy.

The four books under contract were eventually written and published and this agent, a woman, then asked if I had a European literary agent. I replied that I did, but was then informed that her own representative in London was the best in the business, having once represented Sir Walter Scott! She implied that if this agency had been good enough for him it should be good enough for me.

What many would-be writers do not realize is that publishing is a business and that a publisher must be convinced that he can make money by the publication of a book or a magazine article; otherwise he cannot be interested. It is as simple as that.

There was another fact that took a long while for me to learn; this was that even though a subject might hold tremendous interest to me, it might leave editors unimpressed. Too, I discovered that a two-headed calf in the United States holds far more interest than a five-headed calf in Africa. On the other hand, it is difficult to predict just what will interest editors and the reading public. I once photographed a giant water bug in the act of killing an eight-inch snake. This photograph was published all over the world, including Russia. I received numerous letters about it from many countries, but most of them came from readers in Australia. Why this was I do not know.

As a professor I was brought into close contact with other biologists. Too, I had abundant opportunity to find out about anything unusual. Specimens were continually being brought to me for identification and information. These ranged from black widow spiders to Congo eels. Everything of special interest I investigated and photographed. During these years it was amazing the strange things that came to my attention. On the other hand, people would often call me or write me to describe some unusual or amazing creature or plant, and, upon investigation, these usually turned out to be something very common and not unusual at all. One day a local lady, whose name I will not reveal, came into my office and was admitted by my secretary. She stated that her problem was highly confidential and asked that the door be closed. After this was done she asked if a snake, cooked and eaten, would make anyone ill. I told her that I doubted if it would, but asked why she wanted to know. She was very evasive but eventually told me that she had served some guests a batch of cabbage and, after they had left, found the remains of a snake in the pot.

I had noticed that she was carrying a container and so I asked if she had the specimen with her. Reluctantly, she was eventually persuaded to let me see the "stewed" snake. Much to my surprise—and her relief—the "snake" was nothing more than a twisted strand of plant fiber that had been in the head of cabbage.

People were always bringing specimens to my office for identification. Thus, I was not surprised one morning to find a gallon jar sitting on my desk. It contained a live, slender snake that I did not recognize. I knew, at once, that it was not one of our local poisonous snakes—not a moccasin, rattler, or coral snake —and so I reached casually into the jar and picked it up. In order to identify it I reached for a book and, the snake still in hand, began keying it down. According to the book it was a native of Central America and authorities considered it to be highly poisonous. Needless to say, I returned the specimen to the jar and quickly clapped the lid on. Later I discovered that a man had found the snake in a bunch of bananas and had given it to the janitor, who had put it on my desk. Certainly I should have looked more closely at the snake before picking it up. I had learned something—to be more cautious.

One day in late summer I received an urgent call from a nearby town stating that an eight-foot fish had been trapped in a river, and asking if I wanted it for the museum. Always inter-

This eight-foot sturgeon being inspected by an anonymous bystander was caught in the Tombigbee River. It is the largest fish found in American rivers.

ested in specimens, I told the caller that I would certainly come and see this monster fish. I actually had no idea what it could be.

Upon my arrival I found an eight-foot sturgeon in a stock watering trough. The person who had captured it in a large fish trap was then in the process of charging ten cents admission to view the creature, which was still alive. He had already taken in nearly a hundred dollars, more cash money than he had ever seen at one time. I offered to buy it, but was informed that he was going to have it embalmed and then take it on tour.

The last I saw of the sturgeon it was in a truck headed for a medical school, of all places. Later I heard that the medical school, knowing nothing about embalming a fish, had turned the owner away. By this time the fish was becoming quite smelly in the heat. What eventually happened to it I cannot say, and would rather not know.

I had never seen a garfish before coming to the South and so was very much interested in them. Several times I went seining in one or another of the local rivers, where I often caught tiny specimens about an inch long.

A full-grown alligator gar may reach a length of ten feet and weigh as much as four hundred pounds. They are primitive fish, very closely related to the sturgeons and spoonbill catfish. In a bayou I once saw a six-foot gar rising to the surface, and it reminded me of a surfacing submarine.

Gars, common in Southern rivers and lakes, are unusual and interesting fish. Actually, there are three species, the alligator gar, the short-nosed gar, and the long-nosed gar. The alligator gar is the largest, but the long-nosed gar is the most widely distributed.

Gars are voracious creatures, feeding upon other fish captured by means of their rows of needle-like teeth. Their bodies are armored with exceptionally heavy enameled scales, which are diamond-shaped and set closely together, thus forming a sheath of chain mail. These flint-like scales were once used by Indians in place of stone arrowheads.

On several occasions I seined specimens of one-inch gars and placed them in an aquarium along with other small native fish. I was amazed that even these tiny specimens captured and ate many of the minnows.

Gars are unusual in another respect; they are partly air-breathers. Several times, while seated beside bayous, I have watched them gulping air into their swim-bladders which are modified into a sort of lung. This is an adaptation enabling them to live in warm waters deficient in oxygen.

One day a man came to my office, telling me that the spoon-bill catfish were "rolling" in a nearby lake and that I might be able to obtain some pictures. At the time I knew nothing about these strange fish, but I went with him to the lake. It was a beautiful body of water surrounded by tupelo gums with their enlarged buttresses rising gracefully out of the water.

Selecting a comfortable spot, we sat down to watch. All was quiet on the lake's mirror-like surface, and we waited. After about fifteen minutes I saw a four-foot spoonbill break the water and disappear below the surface again in a graceful curve. Suddenly other spoonbills were "rolling" all over the lake and I got out my camera. By this time the lake's surface was quiet again. Again we waited. After a few minutes another spoonbill broke the surface, followed by dozens of others. This "rolling" activity appeared to be triggered by one individual, followed by many others. Evidently this is related in some way to the fishes' breeding habits. Unfortunately, I was unable to obtain good photographs.

Spoonbill catfish, often known as "paddlefish," are among the world's most unusual fishes. Actually, they are closely related to the gars and are not a type of catfish at all, their chief resemblance to these fish being in the complete absence of scales. The name, spoonbill, is derived from the wide spatulate snout used for stirring up the mud at the bottoms of lakes and rivers to obtain food. The usual size of these fish ranges from 30 to 50 pounds, but a record specimen caught in Louisiana weighed 173 pounds.

The rivers of the Deep South are sluggish and muddy, flowing between banks bordered with dense vegetation: cypresses, buttonbushes, and many other plants. There was one place along the Tombigbee River where I often went to watch the play of aquatic life. It was, and is, remote from civilization and, at one place, I found a spot where I could observe nature as it was perhaps a million years ago. Screened by a dense stand of willows and buttonbushes, I frequently sat for hours, entranced by what I saw.

One hot summer day I made myself comfortable at this spot and waited. Soon the great rounded form of an enormous alligator snapping turtle moved through the shallow water near a sandbar, then crawled slowly out of the water. Across the sand

The wood stork is the only stork native to the United States. It feeds in the water and may soar to great heights.

it ambled, then stopped. After a few minutes, it began digging with its front legs. By then I knew that it was preparing a site in which to lay its eggs.

After more than an hour had passed, the great turtle, whose carapace, or shell, measured nearly a yard across, turned around and began laying its eggs. They dropped, one by one into the shallow excavation. Eventually, the creature turned around and brushed sand over the nest and then returned to the water. Unfortunately, I was unable to reach the site to determine how many eggs had been laid.

While watching the activities of the large turtle, another tableau was in the making. A flock of about twenty-five wood storks alighted upon the broad sandbar and began walking about in the shallow water near the river's margin. These large birds had bare heads and curved bills. As they walked slowly along, they held their heads in the water, dragging their bills through it. I supposed that this was their manner of obtaining the mollusks upon which they fed.

Through my binoculars I watched these ungainly birds for a long while. Here, I philosophized, was living Nature, unchanged and unchanging, a glimpse into ancient time.

After awhile something evidently frightened the wood storks and the entire flock took to the air with much splashing and noise. What surprised me most was that they spiraled up, completely out of sight, vanishing in the hot summer sky and I saw them no more.

Since her marriage to me, Annie Laurie had been subjected to such disconcerting trials as discovering animals of various kinds in her refrigerator where I had placed them for safe-keeping—all the way from tarantulas to frogs. One afternoon, however, she came home to find an adult gray fox chained to the leg of the refrigerator. It had been the heaviest thing I could find in the house.

This "tame" gray fox is one I kept for several months. When released, it darted away and was never seen again.

I have never quite understood the psychology of this fox. Some people living out in the country had been missing chickens and so had set a trap to catch the thief, whatever it was. The next morning their son had gone out to see if the trap had caught anything. Much to his surprise, there was a "pretty dog" in the trap. He released the "dog" and carried it into the house in his arms, the animal making no effort to escape. The father, astonished, told him that the "pretty dog" was, in truth, a fox!

The fox was eventually given to me and, having nowhere else to keep it, I chained it to the refrigerator, using an old dog collar for the purpose. During the following months I often led the fox around my back yard and it seemed quite tame. When I sat down, it would sit on its haunches like a dog and watch me through inquisitive eyes.

Eventually, I decided that my pet should be returned to the wild and so I took it to a deep, forested area and sat down beside it. It was quiet and friendly, as usual, as I slowly unbuckled its collar. Much to my amazement, however, the instant the collar was removed the "tame" fox darted away into the bushes and I never saw it again. Evidently the collar and chain had represented captivity and when these had been removed it was again a wild creature. I suppose it had never been really tame at all.

I had often seen and heard what interesting pets raccoons made, and when a young coon was given to me, I was elated. I kept it in a cage, hoping eventually to tame it and allow it the freedom of the house. Naturally, my wife took a dim view of the idea, but she was tolerant. However, I could never make friends with the little beast. Whenever I approached its cage it would cover its eyes with its front paws and utter loud screams as if I were murdering it. At last, in desperation, I decided to try liberating it in the house, which turned out to be a grave error as I quickly discovered. It darted under a bed and crawled up among the springs. I knew that I had to recapture the creature or face divorce proceedings, and so I crawled under the bed, lying on my back, and tried to grab it. This made the coon angry and it then wet in my face, bringing our "friendship" to an abrupt end. I released the varmint in some nearby woods and never saw it again, nor do I wish to. Pet raccoons may make wonderful and interesting pets to some people, but not to me!

The life of a professor of biological science is filled with many things, some routine, others unique. As time went on I became more and more involved with research problems dealing with insect control and related projects. As ex-officio Director of the State Plant Board, I was in charge of a large organization dealing with plant quarantines as well as insect and plant disease eradication matters. However, my chief interest, by this time, was centered on writing about plants and animals, and I never missed an opportunity of going off to any location where something of interest was occurring. Often such an expedition resulted in a book or a magazine story.

7

THROUGH THE CAMERA'S EYE

I OBTAINED my first camera while still attending Montana State University. For a long while I had been intrigued by cameras and the things they could do in recording nature as seen by the human eye. Most of the cameras I had known would focus no closer than about three feet, too far off for close-ups of most plants and animals.

The first camera was of French make and had been used by the local police for photographing prisoners. It was 9 × 12 centimeters and had a ground glass for precise focusing. Even with this camera, however, I could not get closer than three feet. Fortunately, there was an elderly professor of zoology who was also interested in photography, and he introduced me to supplementary lenses. I was elated to discover that when I placed one of these lenses in front of my camera lens, I could actually record subjects up to natural size, which was exactly what I had been seeking.

About this time I discovered something else. Not having much money for such an expensive avocation, I began experimenting with cheap spectacle lenses from the ten-cent store. I soon found that when I placed one of these lenses in front of

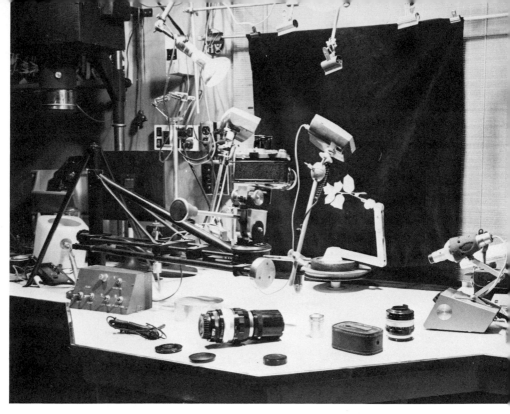

A corner in my photo studio. Here I have recorded many facets of plant and animal life.

Hutchins photographing an oak apple gall

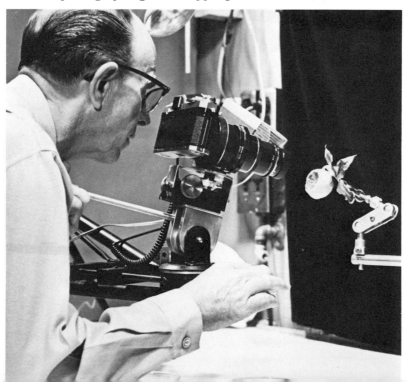

my camera lens, the image size was greatly increased. For example if I used the lens from a pair of spectacles marked 8 (eight diopters), the focal distance from lens to subject was about five inches. This was wonderful and I thought that I had made an original discovery, but I later learned that many others had used this technique.

Having learned something about basic photography, I was soon offered the job as photographer for the Department of Zoology and Entomology at Montana State University. A well-equipped studio and darkroom were available, and I continued to learn techniques. At this time glass plates were being used exclusively; it was several years later that cut film came into common use for view cameras. This was a great improvement both in quality and in reduced weight. While doing work for the department, I also experimented with color photography, a relatively new thing on the photographic horizon. This was a German process and the plates were Agfa color plates. The resulting pictures were of excellent quality.

About the time of my graduation, 35 mm cameras were coming into vogue, but lenses and films had not yet reached the degree of perfection achieved at present, and so I stayed with my 9 × 12 cm camera for several years. A couple of years later I obtained a 4 × 5 Speed Graphic and considered myself really in business. I thought I had become a top-notch photographer. Thus, while attending a science meeting at Atlantic City one time, and seeing a young woman photographing a glass-blowing exhibit, I stopped and offered her a lot of advice. She had an old beat-up Graphic and I assumed her to be an amateur. I am happy to report that the lady took my suggestions good-naturedly. It was not until several weeks later that I learned that she had been none other than Margaret Bourke-White, the famous photographer for *Life* magazine, who had covered World War II from beginning to end.

Gradually I acquired more and more equipment and learned

This daisy was photo-graphed through the eye of a grasshopper. Like other insects, grasshoppers have compound eyes made up of many tiny lenses.

more about using it. Each picture project offered a new challenge. As any biologist knows, insects have compound vision; their eyes are made up of numerous tiny lenses, or ommatidia. Whether an insect, such as a grasshopper, actually sees many images of the same object, or just one, is still not known. However, I decided to attempt to take a photograph through a grasshopper's eye—no simple process. I set up a photomicrographic apparatus having several short-focus lenses. Just below these lenses I placed the carefully dissected-out portion of a grasshopper's compound eye. It was a complex and tricky project and I will not bore you with the details. However, at the end of two weeks I had obtained an excellent series of pictures showing multiple images as presumably seen by a grasshopper. I was very proud of the results and some of the pictures were widely published.

Among my most elusive insect subjects have been dragon-

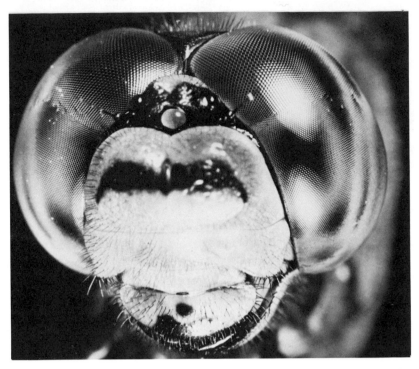

The head of a dragonfly. Notice its many individual eyes and the way the large compound eyes are expanded to enable the insect to see in all directions.

flies. They dart here and there over ponds and streams, rarely alighting, making their photography most difficult. While concentrating on these insects for a book about them, I often spent hours perched beside ponds, trying to record their flight. At last I was successful in obtaining several excellent photographs, one of which was awarded the Best of Show in the photo competition sponsored by the American Entomological Society.

One summer the Smithsonian Institution was engaged in excavating an Indian mound a few miles from my home and asked for my aid, not as a photographer but to identify some of the animal skeletons found along with the ancient Indian remains. Naturally, I took my cameras along to the dig and shot many photographs in addition to helping with the animals,

This prize-winning photograph shows a dragonfly in flight.

finding them to be alligator and turtle remains.

Just about everything imaginable came to my attention at one time or another. Once I was sent the preserved specimen of a six-legged frog from a lake near Memphis. The specimen was that of a leopard frog and it did, indeed, have an extra pair of hind legs. I decided that *Life* magazine would be interested

This six-legged frog was found in a Southern lake. Later, several more of them were captured in the same lake.

and called them. They were interested and asked me to do a photo story. Thinking that an X-ray of the frog would be interesting, I called the local hospital, asking for the X-ray lab. After explaining the reason for my call, I overheard the technician remark to some other person in the lab, "Hutchins wants us to X-ray a damned frog." They did, however, take the X-rays I requested.

We discovered that the six-legged frog was a mutation, not merely a freak. These six-legged frogs continued to appear in the lake for several years. Interestingly, I recalled that the first picture I ever had published had been of a frog with no hind legs at all. It appeared in *Nature* magazine, no longer printed.

There is rarely a dull day in the life of a professor of biological science. One afternoon the sheriff came to my office, along with the coroner and a policeman. They asked that I accompany them out in the country to photograph a "dead baby" for evidence. I assumed it to be a murder case and went along. Upon arrival we were shown a large glass jar containing a preserved human embryo. Obviously, it was an old specimen, apparently sealed in a hospital jar. Someone had unearthed it near a cabin. In this case I took no photographs and we never did discover how the specimen happened to be there.

It was not at all unusual for me to be called upon to take photographs to be used as legal evidence. These have ranged from dead bodies to a rubber boot having a tiny hole burned through it by a high-voltage charge of electricity, causing the death of the man who had worn it.

My wife has a large family, many of whom enjoy the out-of-

Photograph of an io moth taken by the light of fireflies. The fireflies were attached around the edge of an opening in a piece of cardboard.

doors. Soon after my marriage into this family, they established a summer camp on the attractive Luxapillila River, located half an hour's drive from the university. Each individual family group had its own summer cottage. This was before air conditioning and the reason for spending the summers on the Luxapillila was to avoid the heat in town.

This, I found, was a wonderful place to observe and photograph plants and animals, especially insects. Nearby was a sizable lake where many water birds nested, as well as a large cypress swamp inhabited by coons and possums. One summer I devised a combination flash rig and set-camera which, I hoped, would enable me to obtain pictures of some of the inhabitants of the cypress swamp. To the camera was attached a string which would trip the shutter and set off the flash if it was pulled. The other end of the string was tied to some bait placed upon a fallen log. This turned out to be a most fascinating project; each morning I visited the site, hoping that some varmint had tripped the camera. Usually this had occurred and, if so, I could not wait to get back to the darkroom to see what was on the film. I never knew what I'd find. Usually it would be a picture of a coon or possum, but the quality was rarely good because the creatures' rears were generally toward the camera. Why this was I do not know. One morning when I developed the film I was astonished to see a man's image. It was a man I had never seen, but the startled expression on his face had been faithfully recorded. Imagine, if you can, walking through a deep cypress swamp at night and having a photo-flash go off in your face! For all I know the man may be running yet.

My various secretaries over the years have had some interesting experiences and few dull days, and I deeply appreciate their indulgence and fortitude. One was especially brave, even going so far as to aid me in the handling of poisonous reptiles. On one of our western trips, my wife and I were driving down a road in Oklahoma when I spotted a large tarantula ambling slowly across in front of us. Naturally, I stopped the car and was able to capture the enormous spider in a jar. It was near dusk and the local tarantulas were evidently on the move; I saw and captured several more specimens. At this point my wife informed me that I had to make up my mind as to whether she or the tarantulas were going to ride in the car. I assured her that the lid of the jar was very secure and that my specimens could not possibly escape. Anyway, we arrived at the next town and spent the night. There I packed the tarantulas in a box and mailed them to my secretary to be kept, pending my return.

My secretary later told me that when the package arrived, the other girls in the office all gathered around to see what her boss had sent. As may be expected, enthusiasm dropped when the collection of living tarantulas was revealed. Later they turned out to be very cooperative subjects, allowing me to take numerous pictures of them. Eventually this secretary resigned from my employ, not, I hope, as a result of the tarantula inci-

This giant waterbug was photographed in the act of killing an eight-inch water snake.

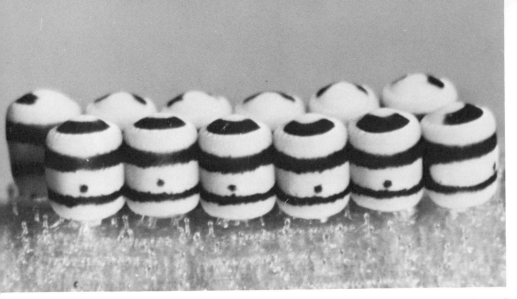

Insect eggs make interesting photographic subjects. Greatly enlarged eggs of the harlequin bug resemble tiny barrels.

dent. She did, however, travel as far away as possible, taking a position as a confidential secretary in the U.S. Embassy in Tokyo, Japan. She later served in embassies in Turkey, Belgium, and the Philippines. I am sure that she has had some interesting experiences but I doubt that she has been involved again with poisonous snakes and tarantulas.

One day, at our summer camp on the Luxapillila, I discovered a three-inch giant water bug in a life-and-death battle with an eight-inch water snake. The large insect had grasped the snake in its raptorial forelegs and had probably "stung" it with its poisonous beak. The snake still struggled but was partly incapacitated.

I scooped the specimens up in a bucket and, later, transferred them to an aquarium where the insect still retained its hold on the snake. Thus, I was able to obtain an excellent series of photographs, some of which were widely published. I received letters concerning the insect-snake combat from many parts of the world.

During these years I viewed many strange and interesting things through my camera lenses. These ranged from a giant

Close-up of African driver ant. A type of army ant, these driver ants may kill a large animal if it is unable to escape them.

walkingstick insect, the largest insect in North America, to tiny insect eggs, many of which showed remarkable forms and sculpturing under high magnification. I wrote a book about seeds and these, too, were a challenge, since great magnification was needed in most instances.

Challenging also was the photography of African driver ants

Army ants stream through the jungles of Central America in large numbers, remaining in one place for only a short time.

Australian bulldog ants are vicious. They dwell in eucalyptus forests and rush out of their underground nests to attack enemies.

Photo rig for close-up photography of plants and animals. Most of my close-up pictures in recent years were taken by means of this piece of equipment which has two electronic flashes moving synchronously to focus on nearby subjects. It is especially useful for living subjects, and was constructed and patented by me. (U.S. Patent No. 3,374,342)

and bulldog ants of Australia. Panamanian army ants were photographed on their jungle forays.

I built and patented a device to focus my electronic flash rigs upon close-up subjects and this was very helpful. Almost all my later pictures of plants and animals were photographed with the aid of this piece of equipment.

Always, it seemed, my cameras were poking their inquisitive noses into Nature's secrets, revealing at close range the remarkable details of the amazing world around me.

8
TIME OUT FOR WAR

MILITARY OPERATIONS require specialists in many fields. During World War II in the Pacific theater, for the first time, our forces were faced with several insect-borne disease problems. The chief of these was tropical malaria but there were others, including dengue fever. Fighting in the jungles of Guadalcanal and other South Pacific islands resulted in problems unique to our medical experience. It was not surprising, then, that I should eventually find myself with a commission in the Medical Corps of the U.S. Navy as an Epidemic Disease Control Officer.

I reported for duty at a Navy base in the South, but the senior medical officer was somewhat mystified as to what my duties should be. Apparently there was not much of a local malaria problem, or any other problem involving insect pests. Thus, I was placed in charge of all immunizations on the base. This was foreign to all my training and experience, but fortunately I was able to carry out my duties adequately.

Six or seven miles off the Gulf Coast lies Cat Island, several miles long and half that in width. This bit of land is heavily forested and is the haunt of alligators, raccoons, and snakes. It was named "Cat Island" because the original Spanish settlers considered the coons to be a type of cat. On this island the U.S. Cavalry had established a war dog training base. Unfortunately, the island was heavily infested with mosquitoes which transmitted heart-worm disease from dog to dog. In some way the commanding officer had discovered that the Navy had a professional entomologist on duty in the area and so requested that I visit the war dog base and advise them about their problem.

I was met at the dock at Gulfport by a cabin cruiser, fancy with polished brass and shining woodwork. Greeting me aboard was a cavalry captain in shiny boots complete with spurs. We headed out across the Gulf and I perched on the bow watching a couple of porpoises cruising just ahead of the bow wave, as is the habit of these animals. Arriving at Cat Island, I found an extensive cavalry post under the command of a British colonel who fulfilled all my conceptions of what an old-time British cavalry officer should look like. I was treated royally and enjoyed an excellent meal in the tent mess hall, after which the post surgeon and I boarded horses and rode around the island. I suppose that the U.S. Horse Cavalry is no longer in existence and so I am pleased to have had this brief experience with this military organization whose long and illustrious service has played such an important part in our history. At this post the cavalry sergeant was in charge of sixteen saddle horses.

On our ride around the island we passed many small ponds, all surrounded by dense jungle. Alligators of all sizes were abundant and their tracks were common in the muddy areas. Mosquitoes were, of course, present in large numbers. I made several suggestions as to ways of mitigating the heart-worm problem among the war dogs, but I do not know if any of them proved effective, since I soon found myself on the other side of the world concerned with other problems.

One day I received orders to report to Chief of Naval Operations in Washington, D.C. Upon arriving in Washington and reporting for duty, I was sent to a small department of the Navy called the Interior Control Board. There I filled out numerous forms and answered endess questions. Apparently the chief things they wanted to know were, could I paddle a canoe and could I ride a mule? This time I was mystified.

The Interior Control Board seemed to be a small, hush-hush organization. There were maps upon some of the walls, all covered with drawn shades. I was informed that I would be going to Calcutta by air and would be staying for a time at the Great Eastern Hotel. I was then ordered to report back in two days.

Returning to the Interior Control Board office two days later, I was seated in a room with half a dozen admirals who began telling me what my work would be. It seemed that there had been reports that the Japanese were spreading bacterial diseases by air, especially in China. It would be my duty to travel to China over the Burma Road and accompany the Chinese army, attempting to determine if bacterial diseases were actually being dropped from Japanese aircraft. I was informed that I had been especially chosen for this assignment because of my experience and training. Just how I was to carry out this assignment was left completely up to me, and I at once thought of a serious difficulty: I knew not a single word of Chinese.

At the end of the meeting I was advised to think the matter over, and the meeting was adjourned. I did, indeed, think the matter over and the following day returned to the Interior Control Board offices, telling them that I did not think that my experience and training fitted me for the assignment, since I was actually an entomologist and not a bacteriologist. This apparently gave them some food for thought. They then asked, "Isn't an entomologist about the same as a bacteriologist?" I explained the difference, pointing out that an entomologist deals with insects, while a bacteriologist deals with bacteria. This seemed to be news to them.

Two days later I received a call at my hotel, stating that I

A "fighting Marine." Even though I was in the Medical Corps, I was required to wear full fighting uniform while on Guam.

was being ordered to the Pacific, to an island designated only as Duva, where there was an outbreak of dengue fever, a mosquito-borne disease. This assignment was more to my liking and I reported to the U.S. Navy at San Francisco. After a delay, as usual, I was ordered to board ship for Fray, which, as everyone knew—including the Japanese—was the code name of Hawaii.

I traveled by aircraft carrier to Pearl Harbor and again waited, this time for two weeks—which was fine with me, since it gave me ample opportunity to see and enjoy these beautiful islands. I also visited the excellent Bernice Bishop Museum. By this time I had learned that Duva was the code name for Guam and I thus knew exactly where I was going. Guam, at this time, was a "forward" base, deep in enemy waters, and our jumping-off place for Japan.

I was eventually handed orders to board another carrier, the

Copahee, headed for Guam. After a few days at sea we ran into heavy weather and soon entered a typhoon. The small carrier bucked like a bronco as we followed a zigzag course to confuse any lurking submarines. Flying fish were numerous and each morning I collected several specimens that had sailed aboard during the night. Examining their stomach contents, I found very little evidence of food and I wondered what they fed upon. After the storm had passed, several albatrosses appeared and followed the ship; otherwise the seas were devoid of life.

We crossed the International Date Line on a Thursday and the next day was Saturday. We had lost a day. We passed Eniwetok Atoll about noon, allowing me my first sight of a Pacific atoll.

Atolls are strange islands, usually composed of a central island surrounded by a circular coral reef. As with most atolls, Eniwetok has no central island, it having been weathered away, leaving only the circular exposed reef upon which palms and a few other plants have taken root. Atolls are formed because the corals, being alive, continue to grow, while the central, original, island wears away or submerges. The result is a string of small coral islands surrounding a protected lagoon.

The Pacific is the earth's largest ocean. It appears very large on a map, but to really appreciate its size one must cross it by ship. Days succeed days and one seems lost in an immeasurable vastness of time and distance. Surrounding the ship there is only the sea, the long hill-like swells rolling endlessly against far horizons. As the ship moves slowly southward, new constellations, never seen at home, appear above the southern horizon. Each succeeding night they rise higher and at last the Southern Cross blazes in the sky. Captain Joshua Slocum captured the feeling well in his *Sailing Alone Around the World* (1899). He said, "To cross the Pacific Ocean, even under the most favorable circumstances, brings you for many days close to nature, and you realize the vastness of the sea."

The *Copahee* was now cruising across enemy waters and the ship was blacked-out at dusk. This condition, however, did have one compensation; I was able to study the night skies. A few days later, in the afternoon, we passed the island of Rota, still in the hands of the Japanese. As we watched, a string of bright flashes suddenly appeared on the island, caused by one of our planes from Guam making a bomb-run across it.

Shortly thereafter we discerned the dim blue outline of Guam off our port quarter. The ship passed around the north end of the island and turned southward along its western side and we dropped anchor about dusk in Apra Harbor but were told that we could not be allowed to go ashore until morning. From the deck I could see many details of the island and I was anxious to leave the ship. Night in the harbor was very hot and I was rather amazed to note that the town of Agaña was brightly lighted, even though it was under the very noses of the Japanese. San Francisco, when I was there, had been completely blacked-out.

During the night two Japanese planes flew high above the town, pinpointed by our searchlights, but there were no sounds of antiaircraft fire and no bombs were dropped. I slept in the relative coolness of the flight deck.

With the coming of dawn I could see many of the ravages of war—buildings destroyed and palms clipped off by naval guns during the invasion by our forces several months previously.

Shortly, a boat was made available and several of us passenger officers went ashore. While waiting on the beach for transportation, I noticed many colorful little fish swimming about in a tide pool in the coral reef. This initial observation of the natural history of the island was shortly interrupted when a jeep and a driver appeared and we drove off up the coral road toward Agaña. My driver was also new to the island and so we decided to do some exploring before I was dropped off at my assigned duty station at the 3rd Marine Division Medical Bat-

*A native village on **Guam**. Thatched roofs are ideal dwellings under hot, tropical conditions.*

talion located across the island at Ylig Bay. We drove nearly to the northern end of Guam, stopping now and then to examine the exotic vegetation. Needless to say, I was intrigued by everything I saw. Being new to the Tropics, I saw not a single familiar tree or plant. I did, of course, know a palm tree when I saw one, but that was about the extent of my knowledge of tropical botany. Once, however, I did see a monarch butterfly. It was like seeing a familiar face in a crowd of strangers. Monarchs are probably the world's greatest traveling butterflies; I had also seen them in Hawaii.

We explored all day, covering most of the northern portion of the island. The southern areas were restricted and so we were unable to go there without a permit. Guam is about thirty miles long and half that wide, most of it being heavily forested, except for the slopes of some of the mountains. There are two relatively high mountains: Mount Alutom, 1,125 feet, and Mount Tenjo, 1,020 feet.

Near dusk I decided that I had better report to my new post if I were to have a place to sleep. We drove across the island to Ylig Bay where the 3rd Marine Division was stationed and I checked in. I was welcomed enthusiastically by about twenty medical officers and I soon learned why they had been so glad to see me. In order to fight a war one must first have an Officers' Club and the doctors were in the process of erecting one. They had obtained all the needed parts for a large Quonset hut and were then putting it up, a very laborious job. An additional hand was urgently needed. Thus, they were glad to see me and at once put me to work. My first assignment was to move a couple of six-foot sections of coconut logs over to the building site. In my ignorance I supposed that these logs would be pithy and light in weight. To my surprise, I quickly found that the logs were as heavy as lead. We worked until well after dark before we stopped. This was my initiation into the rigors of war.

Eventually, I was assigned to a tent with a dentist. The 3rd Marine Division had just returned from Iwo Jima and most of the conversation concerned that operation and the trials and tribulations endured there. Apparently, it had been no picnic. I was warned against going about Guam without an armed escort, since there were still several thousand Japs hiding in the jungles.

The next morning after breakfast in the tent mess hall I walked down to the coral reef surrounding Ylig Bay. It was all new and fascinating and I marveled at everything. The tide was out, allowing me to walk out across the reef to the point where the surf thundered over the edge. Upon the outer reef I saw several large slate-pencil sea urchins. They were clinging to the

Slate-pencil sea urchins cling to the coral along the outer edges of the reef. This one is about ten inches across. The heavy spines are dark red.

coral and the surf was periodically bathing them in rainbow-hued spray. They made me think of great jewels in the sun. Just back of the outer reef were many shallow tide pools where I saw hundreds of small reef fishes, arrayed in every hue of the spectrum. There were also some small octopi, all against a background of chromatic coral. Probably no biologist could have been more thrilled than I was, exploring my first tropical coral reef. It was one of the supreme experiences of my life and its memory remains with me, undimmed by time and distance.

Our well-equipped medical laboratory was housed in a Quonset hut located at the jungle's edge some distance above the bay. It was surrounded by great breadfruit and barring-tonia trees. On my first morning I cut a gash in the bark of one of the breadfruit trees and was amazed when a stream of milky sap oozed out and ran down the trunk. I thought that I had discovered a new source of rubber and collected a quantity of it in a beaker and took it back to the laboratory. However, after treating the sap in every way that I could think of, it still retained its gummy consistency and so I concluded that it held no promise as a rubber substitute.

Of my official duties on the island of Guam during the following months I will have little to say. They were mostly routine, allowing ample time for exploration and to study the fauna and flora of this island that was so new and so different.

Dengue fever is transmitted by a mosquito, the same one that transmits yellow fever. We sprayed the island from the air with DDT and the disease situation was soon under control. There was no problem of malaria, but internal parasites were common. One of the most annoying pest mosquitoes was one whose

The large fruit of the breadfruit is often eaten by natives. The trees are common in the forests.

Screw pine, or pandanus, trees are common on Guam. Certain mosquito larvae live in the leaf axils.

larvae lived in the water-filled leaf axils of pandanus, or screw pines. The larvae of these mosquitoes (*Aedes pandani*) live nowhere else.

There were numerous large toads on the island. During rainy periods the ground seemed to be covered with them. Investigation showed that they had been introduced from Central America many years previously, to control insect pests. Whether they had been an aid in this respect I do not know, but I noticed many dead toads in the jungle and wondered what had killed them. By dissecting some of the toads in the laboratory I discovered that their intestines had been punctured by the sharp spines of buffalo treehoppers they had eaten. It appeared to me that the bugs were killing the toads, instead of the other way around.

My explorations of the island were divided between three

areas: the jungle-filled valleys, the mountains, and the coral reefs. Trips into the dense forest and jungle were not without hazards because of renegade Japs hiding there. Almost every time I discovered an interesting place to explore, one of our men would be killed there the same day or a few days later. This happened too often for comfort, but did not hinder my explorations. The jungles seemed so peaceful that I could not believe there was danger there. This was due probably to the illusiveness of the hiding Japanese. Only once did I actually see one of them. I was driving down a road in a jeep and as I passed an old thatched native hut I saw a Japanese soldier dart away and disappear into the bush. He appeared to be unarmed.

Using materials at hand, I constructed a butterfly net and began collecting butterflies. One afternoon I was deep in the forest on the slopes of Mount Tenjo capturing these insects. There are a number of interesting species on the island and, as I walked about, I assumed that I was the only person in the entire Pacific area thus engaged. Much to my surprise, I saw through an opening in the forest another man swinging a butterfly net!

Naturally, we were attracted to each other and I found that he was an airplane pilot whose hobby was butterfly collecting. All during World War II he had collected on many Pacific islands and discovered several species new to science.

About this time I was very fortunate in making the acquaintance of Lt. D. H. Johnson, previously Assistant Curator of Mammals at the U.S. National Museum in Washington. He was then on loan to the Navy to study the mammals and birds of the Pacific area as possible reservoirs of human diseases. He was attached to the Naval Research Unit located on the western side of Guam. He and I often went on short expeditions to various parts of the island, and I enjoyed these excursions because it had been a long while since I had been associated with a fellow biologist. He was interested in collecting and observing the island birds and animals, and so one day we went up the Ylig River, taking field rations and two 410-gauge shotguns.

We followed a trail that skirted the hills and eventually plunged into the jungle, passing through the luxuriant tropical growth where great forest trees towered upward, holding masses of epiphytic ferns and a few orchids. Climbing vines hung from the larger trees and pandanus or screw pines often blocked our way, since their leaves had numerous sharp spines. Progress was possible only by hacking passages with our machetes. In places we were forced to detour around the great column-like root systems of banyans and clumps of wild banana. Thorny lemonchine bushes and ropelike lianas caught at our clothing, slowing down our progress. Overhead, large *Euploea* butterflies, black with blue spots, fluttered through passages in the jungle.

We came eventually to an opening in the forest and, beyond this, found a dim trail that led into a deep canyon where the jungle was even more dense and luxuriant. Here the earth was damp and great aroids towered above us. At one point I saw, only a few feet ahead, a Micronesian kingfisher perched on a limb. Its underparts were orange while its back, wings, and tail were bright metallic green. I had seen these birds before; a pair of them had a nest in a hole in a coconut tree near my tent at Ylig Bay.

The way now led through a grove of barringtonia trees and there were many of their square-shaped nuts strewn upon the earth, some of them sprouting in the damp soil. High above the forest we spotted several fairy terns. As we watched, one of them alighted on the horizontal limb of a large tree and Johnson decided that it must be nesting there. After expending considerable effort and risking our lives, we were able to climb up to the limb where the graceful bird had landed. The bird, of course, had flown away, but there was one egg resting on a flat place on the limb with no pretense of any sort of nest.

Barringtonia nuts contain a narcotic substance used to stupefy fish, enabling the natives to capture them.

Beyond this point the trail disappeared and we were forced to hack our way, foot by foot, through the jungle. We could see only a few feet ahead. I suddenly spotted two fruit doves perched side by side on the limb of a breadfruit tree. These were specimens Johnson wanted for the museum, and so I raised my gun and fired, killing both birds at one shot.

I had seen these birds before, but this was the first time I had been able to examine specimens at close quarters. They were, I found, very beautiful birds, far different from doves at home. Their upper parts were bright metallic green and the tops of their heads were crowned with brilliant red.

There were many more fruit doves in the breadfruit grove and we could hear their calls, which can be described as *toot-toot-toot*, the sounds increasing and decreasing in volume and rapidity.

We climbed up out of the deep canyon and pushed our way over a hill through vegetation so dense that we could see only a

Lt. D. H. Johnson and I ate our lunches in this thatched hut beyond the Ylig River. It is surrounded by coconut trees and (left) a banana tree. The lines running across the picture are military communication lines used during the invasion of Guam.

few feet ahead. Johnson was leading the way and I saw him suddenly jump back and grab hold of a vine. When I reached him I found that he had almost stepped over the edge of a cliff whose sheer face dropped nearly a hundred feet into a deep chasm. Only his quick wits had saved him.

After scouting around, we finally located a trail going along the top of the hill and, when this trail played out, we were forced to climb literally through an area of tangled vegetation where our feet were nearly ten feet above the ground. To a person unfamiliar with the Tropics it is difficult to believe that vegetation may, in places, be so dense and luxuriant as to form nearly solid floors upon which a person may easily walk.

Struggling over such a tangle of vines and trunks, we came eventually to an open glade in which stood a deserted thatched hut. Inside this structure the air was very cool, rendered so by the thick thatching. Here we decided to eat our lunches.

As we sat eating, we noticed several small birds flying about the clearing in wild gyrations. They swung in wide arcs from the ground to the tops of the surrounding coconut trees. Johnson identified them as being cardinal honey eaters and desired to obtain some of them for the museum. He shot a couple of them and I got a close-up look at the small birds. They were about the size of a wren, and the color of the males was mostly bright red. Later, I discovered several of their nests constructed of plant fibers woven between the forks of limbs. Each nest contained two eggs. It is an interesting fact that most birds of the Tropics lay only about half as many eggs as do birds of temperate climates.

After leaving the thatched hut—the natives would have called it a "rancho"—we walked along a narrow ridge with precipitous walls dropping down on either side. Abruptly we spotted a covey of pygmy quail on the ground in the short vegetation. No more than half the size of bobwhites, they ran some distance before flying off. Johnson informed me that they had been introduced from the Philippines by the Spaniards, who once owned the island.

From our vantage point on the high ridge we could now look down upon a maze of jungle-filled valleys stretching away toward the distant sea. We could trace the course of the Ylig River from its headwaters in the mountains all the way down to the bay where we could see the white line of the surf along the reef's outer edge. Slightly to our left lay Pago Bay, its waters pea green in the bright sun. Below us, against the green background, we spotted the tiny forms of fairy terns, and upon a distant ridge, a great poinciana in full bloom glowed like living fire.

Slowly we made our way down out of the mountains and approached the bay. By this time we could hear the sound of the breakers pounding upon the reef, mingled with the sonorous tones of the trade winds in the palms along the shore. Even now, in fancy, I often imagine that I can hear the sounds of that far-off place. They are sounds as old as time, as old as the living sea and the tiny islands scattered across the vast expanse of the wide Pacific Ocean.

Most evenings I spent in my tent, working with specimens collected during the day. Usually I was alone, with only a few geckos for company. These little lizards, ranging from three to six inches long, have expanded toes, enabling them to cling to almost any surface. Numerous insects were always attracted to my light and the geckos stalked them. They chirped pleasantly, emitting their *geek-geek* calls, and I had no objection to their presence except for one habit: they frequently laid their large eggs in the pockets of my clothing. Often when I put my hand in a pocket and withdrew it, I found it covered with a gluey mess. To make matters worse, these eggs were sometimes nearing the hatching stage.

There is an old saying that war is mostly waiting, and this was certainly true in our case. We were waiting until the time was right for the invasion of Japan. But that left me ample time to investigate the island's wildlife.

Typical of the many trips I made was one to the northern portion, most of which is a level plateau, about five hundred feet above the sea and surrounded by vertical cliffs and high rocky headlands. The eastern shore is constantly beaten by heavy seas resulting from the trade winds. The western side, by contrast, is more protected and has several shallow anchorages where small ships may safely anchor, except during the mon-

Sea beans (Lens) *are produced by a climbing vine and may float long distances across the ocean and then germinate.*

soon season in later summer. Rising out of the plateau are several low mountains, Mounts Barrigada and Santa Rosa being the most prominent, the craters of ancient, now extinct, volcanoes.

One morning after breakfast one of the doctors and I boarded a jeep. We had full canteens and a container of field rations. We also took along loaded carbines, since the area was known to be the haunt of many Japanese.

The road or jeep trail eventually climbed up the slopes of Mount Barrigada and we stopped the jeep in the deep forest. My companion stood guard while I explored, collecting a number of swallowtail butterflies and a tiny blue species with threadlike tails on its wings. We noticed many bird's-nest ferns growing on various surrounding trees. These ferns take root in cavities in trees, forming large globular masses nearly a foot in diameter. Debris collects in these tangled masses and they

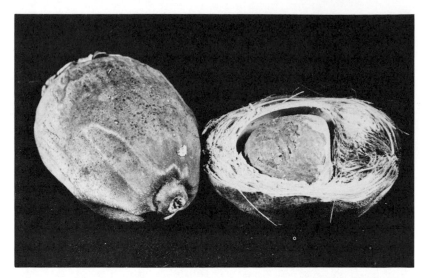

These are betel nuts, the fruit of the areca palm. They are frequently chewed by natives and contain a mild narcotic called arecaine. The one at the right is cut open to show the nut.

eventually become the abodes of snails, ants, and various other insects. I climbed up to examine one of these ferns and collected several animal specimens from them.

Returning to the jeep, we continued on up the slope. All along the way the jungle reached completely over the road, the surrounding area beneath the forest dimly visible in the half-light. There were twisting and climbing vines trailing upon each other, as well as up the trees in a silent struggle for sunlight. One of the most interesting of the trees was the kapok with its great buttressed roots extending away from the trunk like low walls. High above I could see the tree's fiber-filled pods.

We continued on up the so-called road and at one point I noticed a matted tangle of vines at the base of a tree. I stopped to investigate and found that it was the thorny mass of a spiny yam, a plant that has evolved one of the most remarkable methods of protecting itself I have ever seen. This yam, or tuber, grows just beneath the surface, with a tangled mass of spiny vines above the ground. Running up the tree, it sends a leafy vine to the sunlight far above. The tuber, protected by the spiny growth, is relished by the natives.

The road became worse as we progressed. Everywhere the earth was stony and rough, and the day was hot. We stopped the jeep in a shady spot and got out. My companion stationed himself a few feet away, his carbine at the ready. We looked around at the tropical vegetation, but there seemed to be nothing of special interest. Then we heard a slight sound coming from a dense clump of bushes. The doctor snapped off the safety of his carbine and waited. I suppose we were both a little frightened, but nothing was seen. The seconds seemed like minutes. I fully expected to see about twenty Japs come rushing out or to hear the sound of rifles. At last, out of the dim light of the jungle there stepped a large buck deer with fully formed antlers. He regarded us a moment, then bounded away into the forest. It was a pretty sight and the only deer I saw during my stay on the island. These deer are not native; they were introduced by Don Mariano Tobias, Spanish governor of the Mariana Islands from 1771 to 1774, and they have adapted well to the lush tropical habitat.

By this time it was noon. The air was hot and steamy as we stopped the jeep and sat down on a log to eat our field rations and drink from our canteens. As we sat quietly eating I noticed an iguana nearly three feet long slowly climbing over the ground. Less than thirty feet away, it paused and regarded us with unblinking eyes. After a few moments it began moving its head from side to side, then turned and made off through the undergrowth. From overhead we could hear the loud chatterings of birds as they followed its course away through the jungle.

After the iguana had gone we continued on up the road, coming eventually to the brink of the plateau's northern end. Here the vertical wall of stone dropped down about a hundred feet to the fringing coral reef and the white surf that pounded upon it.

The reef extended out from the mountain wall perhaps a hundred feet and, at one point, there was a hole in the reef out of which a fountain of water sprouted more than twenty feet into the air each time the surf beat upon the reef's outer edge. It was spectacular, reminding me of Old Faithful geyser. Evidently there was a natural passage, connecting the spout hole with the sea.

Off to the north and low on the horizon we could just discern Rota, the island my ship had passed on our way around the northern end of Guam.

The next morning at breakfast I was greeted with the news that one of our Marines had been shot by Japs on the slopes of Mount Barrigada the day before. This, to say the least, was disturbing, and I decided that in the future to be even more careful. However, there was not much I could do; it was either go where I wanted to and take the risks or remain in the vicinity of our military encampment. The fact was that most of the Japs hiding in the jungles were unarmed. One day while deep in the forest up on the slopes of Mount Tenjo I came upon a native Chamorro at his thatched hut. I asked him if he ever saw any of the Japs and if so, did they have guns? He replied, "No guns, only hungry."

The truth is that numerous Japanese soldiers, who had taken to the jungles when the island fell to the Americans, remained in hiding for many years after the war was over. One of these, never convinced that hostilities were actually concluded, remaining in hiding for nearly thirty years!

In late summer the rainy season arrived and soon most of the roads, poor at best, turned into quagmires. This forced me to confine most of my explorations to the coral reef. However, this did not really bother me, since the reef and its varied inhabitants were extremely interesting. Each afternoon I took my div-

Spear-fishing on the coral reef of Guam. With goggles and spear it was possible to capture many of the beautiful reef fishes.

ing goggles and hurried down to the shore where I lay face down in the clear water, allowing the current to carry me along about six feet above the submerged reef. Below me a fantastic panorama slowly passed before my eyes. Fishes of every hue of the rainbow darted here and there, most of them protectively colored or marked in some way. Some had eyespots on their tails, probably to confuse enemies as to which ends were their heads. There was one species whose coloration I could not explain from the standpoint of protective coloration. It was black with concentric white rings on its body. It seemed to me that this fish—I called it the "target fish"—was so marked as to actually attract predators. Once I saw what I thought was a dead leaf floating aimlessly through the water. However, when I

Fishes of a tropical coral reef are colorful and have interesting markings. The one I called the "target fish" is near the center.

attempted to pick it up, it darted away. Here was a reef fish camouflaged to resemble a dead leaf. This mimicking coloration I could understand, but there were numerous other reef fish whose markings I could not rationalize as having protective value.

One group of reef fishes, the blennies, were specially interesting. They are perhaps three inches long and dig burrows in the coral sand. Usually there would be a pair living in each burrow. They rested upon the heap of sand in front of the burrow entrances, but at the slightest alarm would turn around and dart into the safety of their burrow. There was another type of blenny that dwelled in shallow tide pools and whose habits made no sense to me at all. Whenever I walked by one of these tide pools the blennies would hop out onto the surrounding coral rocks and perch there until I had passed on by. This was certainly not a fishlike habit and I fail to understand it.

The Ylig River emptied into the bay not far from my tent and was fringed with mangroves and nipa palms. The mangrove roots curved down into the water like the legs of great spiders. This was the habitat of many mangrove hoppers, sometimes called mud springers. These are six-inch fish that have adapted themselves to an air-breathing habit. They perch upon the mangrove roots well above the water but hop off into it when alarmed. One day I was able to capture one of these strange little fish and, since I had nothing better to place it in, I put it in a dry cardboard box. When examined several hours later it was perfectly happy and posed for me in a dish while I made sketches of it. These peculiar fish also occur near the mouths of streams along the southern coasts of Asia, as well as in Polynesia

The mangrove hopper is probably the world's most remarkable fish. It perches on mangrove roots well above the level of the water. This one is about four inches long.

and Micronesia. Their technical name is *Periophthalmus koel-reuteri.*

The use of the scientific name for the mangrove hopper brings up an important point. I am often asked why biologists use Latin names for plants and animals when common names would be so much easier for most people to use. The truth is that common names vary from locality to locality and from country to country. By contrast, the technical name of a plant or an animal is a standard, precise designation, understood by biologists all over the world. When I began studying the beautiful reef fishes of Guam I was able to identify only a few of them, since I had little literature on the subject. Then, one day, I came into possession of a Japanese book having excellent color plates of almost all of these fishes. The book had been found in a hut and a machine gun bullet had pierced one corner. However, it was in excellent condition. All the text and common names of the fishes were, of course, in Japanese but, for each fish, there was given the Latin name. Thus, I was able to identify most of the colorful reef fishes I saw and collected. Without the Latin names the book would have been useless to me.

Often at night I heard rustling noises in the tops of the coconut palms above my tent. For a long while I was mystified, then discovered that the sounds were made by fruit bats or flying foxes. On clear, moonlit nights I frequently saw them on the wing. For bats, they are quite large, measuring nearly three feet across. They have a most disagreeable odor but are eaten by the natives, who call them *fanihis.* One day I obtained a good look at one that was dead on the beach.

Thus, my months on the island of Guam passed pleasantly in spite of the proximity to war. Almost every night Japanese planes flew high overhead, but they dropped no bombs and so were largely ignored. Then came the atom bomb and, abruptly, the war in the Pacific was ended and we made preparations for going home.

On my last night at Ylig Bay I sat in my tent, listening to the sounds of the island jungle mingled with the thunder of the surf upon the reef and of the trade winds in the palms.

The next day, as my ship set course toward the east, the outline of Guam slowly receded into the haze of distance, then dropped below the horizon, and I turned my eyes and thoughts eastward toward Hawaii and home. I realized that one of the most fascinating chapters of my life had ended.

9
SMALL EXPEDITIONS

THE WAR being over, things settled down once again to more routine matters. In addition to teaching and administrative duties, my time was increasingly devoted to writing books and articles and to making small expeditions to interesting places in search of photographs and material. The photography of plants and animals had been my first love, and I now found more time to spend in this field. Some of these short expeditions were made on assignments for the National Geographic Society and for *Time* and *Life*. Others were made on a free-lance basis.

Ants and their habits have always interested me, and over the years I have studied them and written about them, probing into their lives and recording their habits on film. Several of the world's most interesting ants are native to the Southeast and I missed no opportunity to observe and study them.

One of the most remarkable of our native species are the *Colobopsis* ants, close relatives of the large black carpenter ants often seen in rotten logs. *Colobopsis* ants dwell in tunnels in living white ash twigs or in the twigs of other trees. The remarkable thing about them is the fact that the heads of the soldier caste are pluglike and used as stoppers, or living doors,

158

Colobopsis ants live in tunnels in twigs. The soldiers have plug-shaped heads used to close their nest entrances, like living doors. Note the head of one soldier in the nest entrance.

to close the circular entrances to their tunnels in the twigs.

Colonies of these ants live in the twigs, making small entrance holes into them. Here, secure within the living twigs, they rear their young. At all times one of the soldiers stations itself at the entrance with its stopper-shaped head completely closing the hole. Using close-up lenses, I was able to record the activities of these ants.

There is another ant, often found in the Southeast, with an equally interesting habit but of a different sort. This is the harvester ant (*Pogonomyrmex*) that gathers seeds and feeds upon them. Closely related and similar in habits to these ants are the harvester ants of the western Great Plains. On the plains, the colonies are easily spotted, since they consist of

Harvester ants live on Western prairies where they build these large conical mounds.

These are adult harvester ants in one of their underground chambers, along with seeds gathered in the surrounding area.

Here is a harvester ant pulling a small stone out of its nest entrance. The stone weighed fifty times as much as the ant.

high, conical mounds surrounded by bare, circular areas.

Harvester ant workers are highly industrious, gathering and storing large quantities of seeds collected in the vicinity. It was a closely related ant that so intrigued King Solomon that he advised the sluggard to consider her ways.

The harvester ants of the Southeast have a soldier caste with very large heads and powerful jaws, and it is apparently the duty of these large-headed ants to cut up flinty seeds to enable the other members of the colony to eat them.

I photographed the activities of harvester ants in various habitats, including the Great Plains of eastern Colorado. Wherever these ants occur, their storage instincts are highly developed. Often I found nearly a cup of seeds in a single colony.

One of the most unusual food storage methods used by any creature is that evolved by western honey ants (*Myrmecocystus*). These remarkable ants range from Idaho southward into Mexico, where they dwell underground, gathering the honey-like secretions of oak galls. These galls are formed on the leaves of oaks by tiny wasps that live inside them. It is the ants' method of storage, however, that is of special interest. Certain of the worker ants in each underground colony serve as living storage tanks for the honeydew collected from the oak galls. These ants, known as repletes, never leave the nest. They receive the collected honeydew from the field workers and, as a result, their abdomens gradually swell to the size of grapes. In this state they are almost incapable of movement.

In order to understand why this type of storage is necessary one must comprehend the ants' habitat and the special conditions under which they live. Usually they occur in areas of deficient rainfall, where their food supplies become available for only a short period of the year. This is in late summer; thus, the ants must have a means of storing the liquid food upon which they live. Harvester ants, as we have noted, store seeds, which pose few storage problems. The honey ants, on the other hand, gather liquid food, which is another matter entirely; liquid food is difficult to store.

I received an assignment from the National Geographic Society to go to Colorado to obtain pictures of honey ants and to do a story about them. The best location, I found, was in the Garden of the Gods near Colorado Springs.

My wife and I arrived on the scene and located some colonies of the ants along a sandy ridge. About this time a police car drove up and the patrolmen wished to know what we were up to. Someone had reported that we were disturbing the local vegetation.

This occurrence has been a common experience with us. It is one that often takes place when any unusual activity, such as

The Garden of the Gods in Colorado was visited to obtain photographs of honey ants. These unusual ants have their underground colonies along the sandy ridges.

Honey ants gather honeydew from oaks, and certain individuals in the nest take on the task of storing the liquid food in their bodies. This replete has its abdomen swollen with honeydew.

ours, occurs. I have been investigated both by local police in many places, as well as by the FBI. This latter organization thought I was a spy!

After explaining our mission to the Colorado Springs police, they were most cooperative, telling us to go ahead and do anything we wished. I informed them that, in order to obtain the needed photographs, it would be necessary to dig a hole, to get my cameras down at the proper level to view the ants in their tunnels. They approved.

Early the following morning we arrived and located a suitable colony near the top of a ridge and I began digging. The earth was hard and the sun had already heated the barren hills. It was hard work but I persisted, eventually excavating a cavity about three feet deep. Then, with a small trowel, I broke into the ants' nest tunnels. There a most amazing scene was revealed. Within the tunnel, perhaps two inches from floor to roof, were suspended several dozen replete ants, their spherical abdomens glistening in the morning sun. They, of course, made no effort to escape, since they are capable of but little movement. Excellent photographs were easily obtained.

I have often wondered just what the police thought when they saw the enormous cavity I had excavated. However, they had given their approval, and it had all been in the interest of science—or so I philosophized. In any case, the story was a success.

It is always of interest to find an animal, especially an insect, having habits similar to our own. There are, for example, certain ants that actually cultivate gardens for the production of their food. Two kinds of such ants are native to the United States.

Ranging as far north in eastern United States as New England are small fungus-growing ants known to science as *Trachymyrmex*. Rarely noticed by most people, these ants

Trachymyrmex ants cut sections out of leaves and carry the fragments into their underground nests where a special fungus is grown on them. These ants range as far north as New England.

excavate cavities in the ground about the size of an orange. These cavities are usually located a couple of inches below the surface and contain a gray, spongy mass of fungus. This fungus is found only in the ants' nests and it is upon its fruiting bodies that the ants feed.

These little ants are covered with short spines and are rather slow-moving. As nourishment for their underground fungus garden, they gather plant fragments or cut small sections from flower petals or leaves. These are carried into the nests and placed in the growing fungus. In a sense, they are mushroom gardeners, since their fungus belongs to the same fungus family as ordinary mushrooms. I once kept a colony of them in my studio for nearly a year, furnishing them flower petals as compost for their fungus garden.

Even more remarkable than those ants are the large leaf-cutting ants (*Atta*) that are common in the American tropics but which range as far north as Texas and southern Louisiana.

I had been aware of the presence of these ants in Louisiana for several years but had never seen them or their activities. Then, one summer, when my duties allowed my absence from the university, my wife and I loaded equipment and took off for southwest Louisiana. I had made contact with a man I knew there and he had informed me by phone that the ants were then active.

Arriving at De Ridder, Louisiana, we checked into a motel and then went out to locate the ants. We were met in the deep forest by my friend, who showed us an area about a hundred feet square and covered with mounds of excavated earth. In places the ground had settled, due to the caving-in of the large underground nest cavities located five or six feet below the surface. Such areas, my friend informed me, were known locally as "ant towns" and the ants themselves as "town ants."

This is one of the ants' underground fungus gardens. The cavity was about the size of an orange.

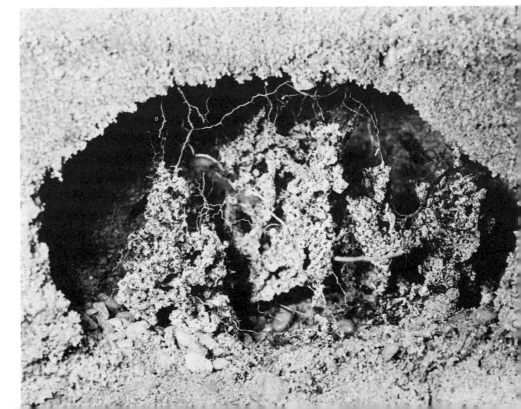

However, we saw no ants; they were apparently all underground in their nest cavities and would not be active above
ground until about dusk.

After supper we returned to the forested area and located the
ant town. Scouting around we located an ant trail. It was about
three inches wide, meandering away through the vegetation.
No ants were in evidence as yet, but I set up my photographic
equipment and waited.

It was becoming quite dark in the deep subtropical forest
and now and then we heard the hoots of owls. Several times I
turned on a flashlight to see if the ants had started emerging
from the one-inch hole at the end of the ant trail. I had about
despaired when I saw the first ant emerge from the hole and
hurry away down the narrow path. Soon other ants appeared,
and within a few minutes they were streaming out in large

Closely related to the smaller Trachymyrmex *ants are the tropical
leaf-cutting ants* (Atta). *Here a column is carrying leaf sections
down an ant trail toward the underground nest. The cavities where
they grow their fungus are nearly a foot across.*

numbers, scurrying along as if driven by some unseen force. I began taking close-up pictures.

We watched and photographed the ants for nearly an hour as they made their way into the forest. Eventually some of them began returning, now carrying dime-sized fragments of leaves held vertically over their heads. Within a short time the traffic along the trail had completely reversed; all the ants were now hurrying back toward the nest. As far as my flashlight would reach up the trail I could see endless numbers of the ants, all toiling along over the uneven trail as if their lives depended on reaching the nest's entrance within a given time. It was an eerie scene there in the deep Louisiana forest. All the surrounding trees were draped with streamers of Spanish moss swaying gently in the slight breeze. Finally the column of ants diminished in size and at last only a few stragglers could be seen. The show was over for the night and so we packed up our equipment and returned to our car parked on the nearby road.

The next morning I returned to the scene, bringing a man with a shovel to help me. We set to work. Fortunately, the earth was sandy and the digging easy. Soon we had a cavity almost large enough to hold an automobile. We had avoided breaking into the ants' subterranean tunnels, but now we carefully began digging toward the point where we judged them to be.

Abruptly our shovels broke into a large cavity about eighteen inches long and nearly a foot high. It was completely filled with gray ant fungus, spongy in nature and honeycombed. Within this mass of fungus were countless worker ants of various sizes, all apparently at work tending the growing fungus. Here and there within the fungus were leaf fragments, probably those collected the previous night.

We carefully dug away the surrounding sandy soil, revealing passages leading to other large cavities, all filled with flourishing fungus, and I could not help thinking about the large num-

The jaws of a worker leaf-cutting ant are scissor-like and used to cut sections out of tree leaves. The leaf sections serve as a compost for their special fungus.

ber of leaf fragments needed to keep these fungus gardens growing. While these pieces of leaves may appear small to us, they are heavy loads to an ant. Some of these leaf fragments were once weighed, as well as the ants that carried them. It was determined that each ant was carrying about eight times its own weight. This is perhaps equivalent to a man carrying a thousand pounds, and at a fast trot. We explored the forested area near the ant towns and saw several trees that had been almost completely defoliated by the industrious ants, making them of considerable economic importance.

So many interesting things came to my attention that I often wonder how I was able to carry on my duties at the university.

At the slightest excuse I would take off on some wild goose chase to investigate some phenomenon or other. I had often read or heard of "rains of fish" but did not really believe that such things were possible. Such a thing seemed too farfetched to believe. However, I read about such an occurrence at Marksville, Louisiana, and decided that it was worth investigating, since a fisheries biologist had been present when it had alledgedly taken place. Naturally, I wanted to investigate it firsthand.

Upon my arrival at Marksville, I began interviewing the local people who had been present. As a result, I was soon convinced that fish do, at times, rain from the sky. This fish "rain" had occurred between seven and eight o'clock in the morning. The previous day had been somewhat unsettled but there had been no reports of tornadoes. However, on the morning in question it had begun to rain, and soon fish of several kinds, all common in the rivers and lakes in the surrounding area, began falling in the streets. These included sunfish, large-mouth bass, and hickory shads. One storekeeper informed me that he had picked up a bass measuring over nine inches long. A U.S. Government fisheries biologist, Dr. A. D. Bajkov, was eating breakfast in a local restaurant at the time and rushed out when informed that fish were raining from the sky. He was able to collect some of the still-living specimens. He later published an account of the incident in *Science* for April 22, 1949.

Naturally, I often took vacations but most of them were devoted to the pursuit of stories about unusual happenings, thus combining business with pleasure.

I had a friend who had a large houseboat on the large Pascagoula River. I had never seen the houseboat or even been into the vast Pascagoula Swamp, which extends northward from the Gulf Coast near the mouth of the Pascagoula River.

The so-called houseboat turned out to be a large river yacht

My expedition into the Pascagoula Swamp was made in this luxurious houseboat. Here it is tied up at an island in the swamp.

having luxurious accommodations. I went aboard taking, as usual, a large assortment of photographic equipment. We went down a tortuous bayou and then into the wide Pascagoula River where we turned northward for several miles. Here, beside a low island, we tied up to the trunk of a great live oak. There were several other men aboard and they went fishing, using small boats that had been tied behind the houseboat. I have never been much of a fisherman and so elected to explore the island instead. Making my way ashore, I walked across the island which was perhaps ten acres in area. Here I found myself in a lush, semitropical setting. It was spectacular and picturesque. Great live oaks were everywhere, their limbs all draped with streamers of gray Spanish moss swaying gently in the breeze.

There were many things of interest on the island and I spent most of the afternoon investigating and photographing them. Then, arriving at the island's southern portion, I was most pleased to find that alligators were building nests along the margin among tall growths of marsh plants. One of the nests was then under construction and I surprised a large alligator in the act of carrying a mass of green vegetation in her jaws. She saw me at about the same instant I saw her and splashed into the water, making a loud noise.

There were, I discovered, several other nests along the island's edge, and I stopped to examine several of them. Some were completed and probably contained eggs. They were about two-feet high and covered areas about six or eight feet across. The reptiles had collected green marsh grass and other vegetation and piled it up, burying their eggs in the masses and allowing them to be incubated by the heat of the sun and the warmth generated by the decaying vegetation.

At one point I found a nest under construction and decided to hide behind some large palmettos and see if any alligators appeared. There was, I noticed, a wet path leading down to the

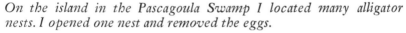

On the island in the Pascagoula Swamp I located many alligator nests. I opened one nest and removed the eggs.

water and so I presumed that the reptile was actively engaged in nest-building.

I waited nearly half an hour, and by this time it was becoming rather dark in the dense forest of the island. Beyond, above the sea of marshland that stretched away toward the south, it was lighter, the sky tinged with a red glow.

I had about given up hope of seeing any activity when a large gator appeared in the bayou. For a minute or so the cow alligator remained stationary, only her eyes and snout above the water. Eventually, assuming that it was safe, she lumbered out of the water toward her nest. She was an ugly beast, at least ten feet long and heavy bodied. She at last reached the nest and lay quietly upon it. After a few minutes she left and disappeared among the stalks of tall marsh grasses. I continued to wait.

A few minutes later she reappeared, this time with a mass of water plants between her jaws. She dropped the plants upon the nest and departed and, since it had become quite dark, I also left and made my way back to the houseboat.

On subsequent days I often returned to the alligator nesting area to watch. Once I made an interesting observation while hiding behind the palmettos. A cow alligator came slowly out of the bayou and crawled upon her nest where she remained for some time. For awhile I was unable to see what she was doing; then I saw that she was voiding water upon the nest. I was still mystified. Later, reading up on alligator habits, I found that the cow alligator regularly voids water upon her nest to keep it from drying out during incubation, a process requiring nearly two months.

Eventually, I realized that our stay at the island was nearly at an end and so I decided to rob one of the alligator nests and take the eggs home with me. I justified my act by assuming it to be in the interest of science. Accordingly, I took a bucket across the island and broke open one of the completed nests. It con-

The alligator eggs were taken home and hatched. Here a young alligator is in the act of emerging from its shell.

tained thirty-six eggs, each one about the size of a hen's egg. While removing the eggs I noticed that the temperature within the mound was perceptibly higher than that outside. Later, I read an account of alligator habits by E. A. McIlhenny in which he had recorded the interior temperature of the nests, finding that they were about twenty degrees higher than outside temperatures. The heat generated by the decaying vegetation raises the interior temperature sufficiently to bring about incubation.

Back at home I placed the alligator eggs in a "nest" on the back porch and tended them as I presumed a cow alligator would. I am happy to report that all the eggs hatched except one. Not a bad record for a foster alligator mother!

As can be imagined, my next problem was what to do with thirty-five baby alligators. In the interest of marital peace I at last decided to liberate most of them in a nearby lake. To me it looked like good alligator territory.

Under wild conditions young alligators are guarded by the

cow for some time, usually until they are nearly three feet long. I placed the little alligators in the lake and they swam away. However, I visited the spot each morning to determine, if possible, how they were getting along. The interesting thing was that none of them could be seen until I had uttered an imitation of a cow alligator's call, "*umph-umph-umph*." At this sound they would come swimming up to my feet where I fed them bits of meat. Apparently at least some of them survived, since several good-sized gators were later seen there.

A few of the baby allligators I donated to the children of friends. This, I quickly discovered, was an excellent way of losing friends. Only a few of the parents still speak to me. One of these is my dentist and I will not be at all surprised if he will, someday, pull a perfectly good tooth just for the fun of it.

This discussion of alligators brings to mind another, unrelated, incident. One of our engineering professors once decided to build a concrete lily pool in his back yard and asked me for my ideas concerning such a pool. When the pool was completed it was most attractive, with tall cattails at one end, pink water-lilies floating upon the surface, and goldfish swimming in the water. About a year later the professor asked me to come and take a look at his pool. When I arrived, he informed me that his goldfish kept disappearing. Even when more were placed in the pool, they mysteriously vanished within a day or two. I examined the pool, noting the healthy appearance of all the plants, and told him that I couldn't understand what had been happening to his goldfish. He replied that it was a mystery to him, since the two-foot alligator he had placed in the pool among the aquatic plants was certainly doing well. I guessed that it was doing well—on a goldfish diet! Engineers, I decided, knew very little about the food habits of alligators.

At one point it occurred to me that a story about mud dauber wasps might be of interest to *National Geographic* magazine.

Among the most interesting of all insects are the predatory wasps. Some capture other insects and store them in their nests after paralyzing them with their stings. Others prey upon spiders and tarantulas.

The mud dauber wasp constructs clay cells on the ceilings of porches and similar places. After the inch-long cells are completed, she then captures spiders and stings them, causing them to be paralyzed. Then she lays an egg in the cell and seals it with more clay. When the egg hatches, the larval wasp feeds upon the paralyzed spiders.

I contacted *National Geographic* and they were interested, so I got to work. In the course of my research on the subject I found that mud dauber wasps were causing difficulty with electronic equipment at the atomic laboratories at Oak Ridge, Tennessee. The busy wasps were building their clay cells in or near the electronic equipment, using radioactive clay gathered from

Mud dauber wasps built these clay cells at Oak Ridge, Tennessee, using radioactive waste. Some were near sensitive electronic instruments, causing them to malfunction. Many of the wasp cells were emitting gamma radiation at the rate of one roentgen per hour.

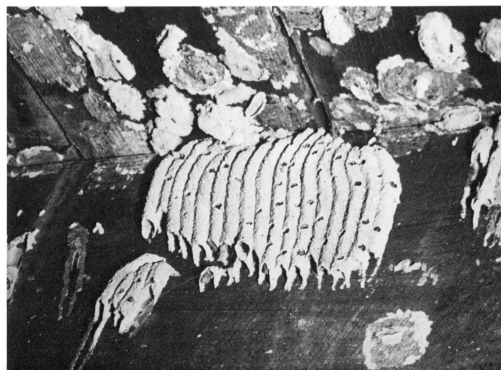

Dr. Alvin F. Shinn, left, and an assistant prepare wasp nesting cages to be pulled across the "hot" disposal pool located just beyond the embankment at the left.

large pools of waste sludge. This, of course, interfered with the proper functioning of the sensitive equipment.

After making the necessary arrangements, I traveled to Oak Ridge where I was equipped with a radiation badge and taken into a restricted zone where the safe permitted time was only fifteen minutes. There were three of us. One man's sole duty was keeping time. The other man was a research entomologist on duty with the Ecology Section. Inside the restricted zone was a large pool of highly radioactive sludge, surrounded by a high earthen embankment. The safe exposure time over this pool was only fifteen seconds! Large boxes, designed to attract mud daubers, were suspended over the "hot" pool, pulled across it on wires. I watched from a safe point outside the embankment while the entomologist examined the boxes. I can assure you that he wasted no time.

Naturally, I wanted photographs and obtained them by raising my camera up over the edge of the embankment and snapping the shutter, then dropping down again. I took a number of shots and the pictures turned out fine. I was concerned lest the film in my camera might be fogged by the high radiation, but it was not.

At the end of the fifteen-minute limit in the restricted zone, we quickly left and returned to the research laboratory where I shot pictures of the work going on there. One of the things they were doing was attaching tiny dosimeters to living wasps in an effort to find out how much radiation the insects were actually being exposed to. What was especially interesting was the fact that one kind of mud dauber wasp apparently could detect atomic radiation and would not use the "hot" clay for nest building. As far as I know, it is the only animal that is able to detect atomic radiation. Certainly, we still have much to learn about wasps and other insects.

A tiny dosimeter has been cemented to an anesthetized mud dauber wasp to determine how much gamma radiation she will receive while building her nest of radioactive clay.

10

INTO THE MYSTERIOUS EVERGLADES

To A BIOLOGIST, the Everglades of Florida are extremely fascinating. Essentially tropical in nature, the southern tip of Florida reaches within one degree of the true Tropics and bears many characteristics of a real tropical region. The area known as the Everglades begins just south of Lake Okeechobee and includes almost all of the region beyond there. Much of it has been drained and "developed," but there are still large areas that have been unchanged by man. Most unchanged is that region included in the Everglades National Park, reaching all the way to the southern tip of the state.

The Everglades received their name as the result of a survey made in the early 1700s by a French surveyor named Gerard de Brahm. He designated the area on his map as "River Glades." Later, on English maps, this was changed to Everglades. The old English word "glaed" or "glade" meant an "open grassy place"—certainly a fitting description of the region. Okeechobee means "Big Water" in the Indian language, and the lake of that name is one of the largest of North America. In former years, before levees were constructed around its lower end, waters from the lake flowed down across the land like a great

A hammock of the Everglades. Upon these high areas grow a wide variety of trees and other vegetation.

grassy river during the rainy season of winter. Scattered over this vast area of saw grass are endless numbers of higher segments of land known as hammocks. This name is of Seminole origin, meaning "a garden place." Upon these isolated hammocks grow an almost infinite variety of plants and trees, flourishing in subtropical luxuriance.

I had been living in the Southeast a long while before getting around to exploring the Everglades. Eventually, sponsored partly by the National Geographic Society, partly by *Time* and *Life*, and mostly by myself, my wife and I went to Florida, making our headquarters either at Homestead or at Naples at different times. It required only one excursion into the nearby Everglades to make me realize just what a fantastic place it was from a naturalist's standpoint. The first trip was in the summer when salt-marsh mosquitoes were so abundant as to make serious photography almost impossible. Even after I had doused myself liberally with repellent, I was able to spend but a short time within the jungle. However, what little I did see filled me with determination to return during the winter when the mosquito season was over.

Accordingly, we returned in January and I was then able to go anywhere I wished, exploring and photographing to my heart's content. I shall never forget the first time I pushed my way through the tall saw grass and onto one of the larger hammocks, perhaps five acres in extent. Suddenly I found myself in semigloom, the sun obscured by dense growths of palms, gumbo-limbos, saw palmettos, inkwoods, wild tamarinds, and other trees in endless variety. Attached to most of the trunks were air plants, some having red or yellow blooms, their colors vivid in spite of the dim light. Upon the tree trunks also grew epiphytic orchids of several kinds, the most abundant being an attractive little species having its lip-petal marked with purple lines. It was *Epidendrum tampense.* The air plants, or bromeliads, were far more abundant than the orchids, festooning the limbs and trunks of almost every tree. Some were very large, their massed foliage making a ball more than a foot in diameter and weighing, I estimated, twenty-five or thirty pounds.

Air plants belong to the pineapple family, as does Spanish moss. All these plants use trees merely as places to grow, drawing no nourishment from them. They are thus epiphytes, not parasites. Water needed for growth is obtained from rain or absorbed from the air, and stored in the axils or leaf bases.

Left: *Epiphytic orchids are common in the Everglades, anchoring themselves to the bark of trees.* Right: *Air plants flourish on almost all the trees. This one will have attractive red flowers.*

The author photographing epiphytic orchids in a live oak. The tree is abundantly draped with Spanish moss.

Often a quart of water may be poured out of a single air plant. Like all plants, they need minerals for growth and these are obtained from dust washed off the tree leaves above.

I climbed up and pulled down a large air plant having several bright red flowering spikes. It contained considerable water and when I emptied it upon the ground I noticed that there were many mosquito larvae as well as some snails.

I pushed on into the hammock's interior, my feet treading over decaying vegetation where numerous pale fungi grew. Once I spotted the tracks of a bear in a marshy place, and in another, the trail of an alligator.

Eventually, I reached the far side of the hammock and saw several egrets wading sedately about in the shallow water. Just beyond them were three purple gallinules. I sat down, entranced by the scene spreading away before me, the attractive birds vividly outlined against the background of tall saw grass waving slowly in the breeze. This was a place, I decided, that a naturalist might dream of but rarely be privileged to see. I set up my camera, attached a long telephoto lens, and began taking pictures.

A snowy egret poses beside a bayou. Egret plumes were once used on women's hats.

The next day I drove down toward Flamingo, located on Florida's southern end, following a road through the heart of the Everglades. I came eventually to Mahogany Hammock where North America's only grove of mahogany trees may now be found. Here grow great mahogany trees, their foliage nearly blotting out the sky. Some of their fruit had dropped to the ground and I found that they contained winged seeds. Near the hammock's edge I was delighted to see a number of heliconid butterflies fluttering about in the sun. These long-winged butterflies are our only representatives of a tropical family, other species being found in Mexico and Central America. I had seen specimens in museums, but this was the first time I had encountered them in their natural habitat.

Above: *A mahogany tree deep in the Everglades. These trees are found only in this area of the United States.*

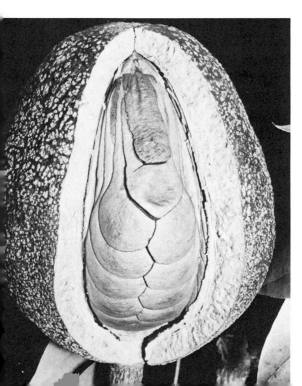

Left: *The fruit of the mahogany tree contains many winged seeds. Here one section of the pod has been removed to expose the seeds. Length of fruit: five inches.*

Above: *A heliconid butter-*
fly, the only member of a
tropical family found in the
United States. Its larvae
feed upon passion flower
leaves.

Right: *A manchineel tree,*
whose sap is highly poison-
ous. It is dangerous to be
under one in the rain. This
one was photographed deep
in the Everglades.

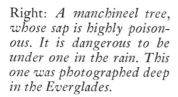

*Armadillos are common. A member of the anteater family, the
armadillo roots in the earth for insects and worms.*

Not far below Mahogany Hammock I saw another large
hammock and pushed my way through the saw grass to explore
it. There were numerous trees, many of which I could not identify. I did spot a large manchineel, probably America's most
poisonous plant. It is reported to have very poisonous and
caustic sap, which causes skin eruptions akin to those produced
by poison ivy but much more severe. It is said that merely
standing under a manchineel tree in the rain can be dangerous.
Its sap was once employed by Carib Indians as an arrow
poison. To be on the safe side, I gave the tree a wide berth and
went on exploring deeper into the hammock, following a dim
trail. I walked slowly along, my feet making little sound on the
soft earth. Thus, I surprised a large armadillo digging beneath
a palmetto. It had heard me but couldn't see me, since these
strange creatures have poor eyesight. I stood still, wondering
what it would do. The armadillo couldn't decide whether to run

or not, or in which direction to go. It stood up on its hind legs and listened; it was aware that some danger was near, but what or where it could not decide. Finally, alerted by my scent, I presume, it darted away through the palmettos at high speed. Its actions had been comical and I chuckled to myself as I walked on down the trail.

Rounding a bend, I came to a small pond where several water birds were feeding. They flew off at my approach and I then noticed a beautiful specimen of shoestring fern attached to the trunk of a cabbage palmetto. If I had not already known about these plants, I would never have recognized this one as being a fern. It looked exactly like a mass of green shoestrings hanging on the side of the tree. Naturally, I set up my camera and photographed it.

A short distance on down the trail, still near the little pond, I was elated to find a beautiful example of a strangler fig growing upon another cabbage palmetto. Later I saw and photographed numerous other specimens of these strange trees, but this first one gave me cause to marvel over its peculiar way of growth. Its trunk was attached to the palmetto and almost surrounded it in a strangling manner. Its name, I decided, was quite descriptive of its style of growth.

The strangler fig (*Ficus aurea*) is a true fig, but begins life in an unusual fashion. When one of its minute seeds becomes lodged on the rough trunk of a tree, such as a cabbage palmetto, it sprouts, sending a stalk upward and aerial roots downward. In time the roots reach the ground and the stalk develops typical leaves. Eventually, the fig grows larger, sometimes almost entirely surrounding its "host" tree, which may eventually die, leaving the strangler fig to grow alone.

There are about eight hundred different species of figs, many of which grow in Florida. One of the most unusual of these is the banyan. I had seen these trees growing on Guam; there was a beautiful specimen located just behind our medical laboratory

Above: *A strangler fig begins life upon the side of a tree where one of its seeds germinates (see arrow). This one is growing on a cabbage palmetto.*

Right: *As a strangler fig grows, it eventually surrounds its host tree and may eventually kill it.*

there. This tree sends down numerous aerial roots from its branches, with the result that it eventually covers a large area, sometimes more than a hundred feet in diameter.

In the Everglades I was pleased to encounter many old "friends" with which I had become familiar on Guam. In addition to banyans, I found crab's-eye beans (*Abrus*). These shiny black and scarlet beans are produced on a small vine that climbs up on trees and other vegetation. These beans are beautiful but contain a very poisonous alkaloid quite similar to that found in some poisonous snakes. The plant grows in many places in the Tropics and, in India, the toxin was once smeared on daggers to bring about instant death. On Guam, one of our medical corpsmen was attempting to pierce some of these pretty beans to make a necklace. The needle he was using accidentally pricked his finger, causing his entire hand to become seriously swollen.

Another "friend" I encountered in Florida was the royal poinciana, or flame tree, which I consider to be the world's most beautiful flowering tree. It has fernlike foliage and a spreading form and, when in bloom, is covered with clusters of scarlet flowers. Seen in a forest, it reminds one of a great scarlet umbrella. At the southern end of Guam I had seen an enormous specimen of this tree, then in full bloom. Many of the petals had fallen to the ground, making it look as if covered by a scarlet carpet. This tree is located but a short distance from a monument erected to commemorate the landing on Guam by Magellan on March 6, 1521. Whenever I saw a flame tree in Florida my mind reached back across the years, and half a world away, to the great poinciana blooming beside the blue Pacific and the surf thundering over the nearby reef.

Most of the shoreline surrounding the Everglades is bordered by mangroves, one of the world's most interesting trees. I first made their acquaintance on Guam where they grew along most of the rivers near where they entered the sea. They have

adapted themselves to fresh or brackish water where they grow
along the shores, their roots curving outward and down into the
water like the legs of great spiders.

While in Florida I had been searching for a place where I
could actually walk into a mangrove swamp, in order to photograph and study these plants at close range. In most places, the
only way to approach these trees is by boat. I found, however,
that Pine Island, just off the West Coast, was an ideal place.
There I could walk in among the tangled masses of mangroves
on dry coral sand, and could study the birds, snakes, tree snails,
and other forms of life. But the truth is that the exploration of a

*Mangroves have been called the "mothers of islands." Their roots
reach out and gradually enlarge the margins of the land. Note the
root-spears hanging from the tree at the right.*

mangrove swamp is a laborious and tedious endeavor. One must crawl in among the intertwined and branching stems or trunks, and progress is slow and uncertain. It is not a place for a person suffering from claustrophobia, since the uninhibited and luxuriant growth seems to imprison the intruder with entwining arms.

Mangroves have been aptly called the "mothers of islands." Always growing along shorelines, their roots arch outward and down into the sea where they attach themselves. Trunks then grow up from these roots and new roots reach outward again in an endless process. Within these massed roots, sediments accumulate and new land is formed. Thus, an island or a shoreline is slowly expanded.

On Pine Island I was able to observe and photograph the mangrove's mode of reproduction. The blooms are pale yellow, giving rise eventually to leathery fruit. This fruit contains a seed that germinates while still attached to the tree. Gradually

Mangrove root-spears drop from the tree and pierce the mud below. There they take root and grow into new mangroves.

Alligators are common in the Everglades. This large specimen was undisturbed by being photographed.

a root, or radicle, grows out of the lower end of the fruit, reaching a length of nearly ten inches. This root is dart-shaped and eventually drops down and imbeds itself in the mud. In time this spearlike root produces another mangrove.

As further evidence of the mangrove's remarkable adaptation, it may happen that these root-spears fall into water too deep for them to penetrate the mud. In this case they float away, carried by the current, perhaps reaching a distant island or shore. As time passes, the root-spear's center of gravity slowly shifts until it floats point downward. Thus, upon arrival at a new shoreline, it penetrates the sand or mud and grows.

A mangrove swamp, I found, was a most interesting place but I soon realized that it was along the swamp's margins that the real "action" was. Here, in the shallow water, were wading birds in great variety as well as alligators that sunned themselves upon the sandbars. One of the most interesting of the birds was the water turkey, or anhinga, having a slender beak and snakelike neck. These birds nest in the mangrove swamps and live upon fish, captured by swimming through the water, using their wings as a means of propulsion.

An anhinga, or snake bird, perches on a tree in the Everglades. These odd birds feed on fish, captured by swimming through water with their wings.

To complete my Everglades explorations I went to the small town of Everglades. From there I traveled by boat into the vast mangrove swamps of Shark River and White Water Bay. Here a boat may pass through endless mazes of narrow channels and passages, a region unchanged and unchanging. In this jungle on stilts is tropical Nature run riot. Here dwell only alligators, coons, and water birds. There are occasional cypresses holding the great nests of eagles. Imagine, if you can, a mass of thriving mangroves hundreds of square miles in extent. It is a place where men may come and go through the narrow channels over which arch the leafy foliage, but the visitors remain only a brief time, leaving wild Nature to her ancient solitude.

I left the Everglades with a feeling that I had been privileged a brief glimpse of a wild and primitive place where plant growth is uninhibited and unchanging in a near-tropical setting, where panoramas of sky and jungle stretch away to far horizons. May it never change.

11

THE GREAT SMOKY
MOUNTAINS

THE GREAT SMOKY MOUNTAINS NATIONAL PARK lies partly in
Tennessee and partly in North Carolina, and is divided approximately down its center by a high divide, the highest point of
which is Clingmans Dome with an elevation of 6,642 feet. The
slopes of these great mountains are ribbed with deep forest-
filled valleys having bright streams flowing down them through
lush growths of rhododendrons, laurels, and numerous other
trees and shrubs. It is a region of great beauty, now mostly
devoid of human habitation since being set aside as a National
Park.

This area was not always thus. Once it was the home of many
settlers who had dwelled and toiled for generations in its forested valleys. They are gone now, leaving only the stone
foundations of their homes over which grow ivy and a few
garden flowers to mark the places where they once lived. Hidden away in several places are cemeteries where loved ones
now rest beneath the soil where they labored. There are ghosts,
I suspect, in these mountains that walk the trails on moonlit
nights, perhaps remembering the long past, of things done and
half-forgotten. They lived, loved, and died where the forests

A logging train at Elkmont in the Smoky Mountains about 1920. These mountains were logged off during the early part of the century, but the forests are now growing back.

now push upward to the sun and where wild flowers bloom each spring. These forests and flowers are visited and enjoyed each year by millions of people, but only a few are conscious of the way the mountains once were. There are now few reminders.

Before the establishment of the park the Little River railroad snaked up the valleys of the western slopes, its purpose to haul away the great saw logs that had been cut there. These trees were of amazing size, flourishing under almost ideal conditions for growth. There were poplars 200 feet tall and chestnuts ranging up to twelve feet through. Due to the near-perfect environment, many trees that are mere shrubs in most localities frequently reach great size here. Buckeyes in these mountains have been known to grow 125 feet high. In most places these latter trees are shrublike.

The streams rush rapidly down from the higher elevations, tumbling over great boulders and spilling into quiet pools where trout move shadow-like across the sandy bottoms. The banks of the streams are often precipitous, flanked by stony barriers, half-hidden beneath great masses of laurels and rhododendrons, their glossy leaves reflecting beams of sunlight slanting down through the surrounding forest trees.

Gone now are the settlers and the railroad, allowing the mountains to revert slowly to their primitive state. Only at two locations in the park do people still live. One is Cades Cove, located near the park's southern end. The other is along Jakes Creek, the place known as Elkmont. The presence of these dwellings represents an effort by the park to preserve small examples of the way of life as it once was. Those whose cottages may be seen at Elkmont are members of the Appalachian Club, a group that has long been dedicated to continuing the old manner of life in the mountains.

View from Fighting Creek Gap in the Great Smoky Mountains, elevation about 3,000 feet.

It has been our good fortune and privilege for my wife, Annie Laurie, and me to have acquired one of the Jakes Creek cottages where we now live for a large portion of each year. Here we have reveled in the solitude and enjoyed the rare opportunity of dwelling close to wild nature in a sylvan setting. From our mountain retreat, whose picture windows overlook the creek, we watch an ever-changing and always fascinating scene. During summer days we may gaze across the stream where a trail follows along the mossy, rock-strewn bank and where the day-active creatures of the mountains are frequent travelers. They show themselves but briefly, disappearing eventually behind the screening masses of great rhododendrons. At night, when the floodlights are turned on, both stream and mountainside spring into view, revealing a new and totally different character. It is then that the nocturnal creatures become active, replacing those that prefer the day. They pass up and down the trail in their eternal quest for food and, perhaps, merely for adventure.

Having grown up in a mountainous area, it was perhaps inevitable that I should become attracted by the Great Smoky Mountains, the nearest ones to my adopted home in the South. In contrast to the "youthful" Rockies, the Smokies are very ancient. They are of pre-Cambrian origin, their stratas having been laid down long before life appeared on earth. The Rockies are higher and their peaks more rugged than the Smokies, whose contours have been rounded and softened by eons of falling water that has slowly eroded their slopes, shaping them into their present form. They rise, tier after tier, into the haze of distance, soft-green and beautiful.

Always at Elkmont there are the sounds of the boisterous stream, but the tones defy description. There are gurgling noises, arising, perhaps, from the water pouring through hidden passages among the rocks. At night the stream emits different sounds, adding further mystery to the scene.

Bright streams tumble down from the higher elevations of the Smokies. This one is Bear Wallow Branch.

A beam of sunlight illuminates a small waterfall on Husky Branch.

Such is Jakes Creek on pleasant days and nights when skies are clear. Often, however, storm clouds drift eastward across the mountains, spilling their loads of moisture upon the forested slopes. This water finds its way quickly into the creek, causing it to rise with astonishing rapidity. At such time the creek takes on a new and almost frightening personality. The once-happy stream then roars down its rocky course, foaming into pools, its sounds amazingly intensified. But these periods of high water are but small incidents, short-lived. Soon the waters recede, tumbling as usual down from the mountains where the stream has its genesis.

The feeling of contentment while beside Jakes Creek often leads to introspection. This is especially true on summer days when mountain breezes flow gently down the valley and a sense of peace prevails. Today I watch the tumbling waters of the stream, noting how the boulders of its bed are rounded, worn down by millions of years of rushing water. How long, I wonder, does it take the stream to cut away an inch of stone? The water-borne sediments act like a sandblast, slowly wearing and shaping the contours of the sedimentary stones and boulders. If I could see this small stream a hundred years from now I wonder if I could detect many changes. Probably not, because the wearing-away process operates very slowly. Most evident, no doubt, would be changes in the boulders' mottled coverings of lichens and mosses. A century is but an instant of geological time.

This has been the history of these ancient mountains and their time-washed boulders: slow-motion change with, now and then, abrupt alterations during brief intervals of geological activity. A million years may elapse in these mountains, leaving behind little evidence of their passing because the mountains were already old when dinosaurs roamed the earth.

Often in autumn the valleys in the Smokies are filled with fog.

On this summer day I look beyond the stream where the jungle-like wall of the mountain forest begins. There are trees of great variety, as well as vines and shrubs. The great rhododendron beside the bank is now in full bloom, its pale-pink flowers clustered among the dark-green leaves. Upon the banks are bluets, their delicate blooms starring the background of green mosses. Some of the plants and flowers I see have much longer histories than others, but their stories all go far back in time's dim mists. Each one has resulted from living forces thriving in the equitable climate. Yet they can all trace their ancestry back to a common parentage. Back beyond the ancestry of the flowering plants there were the mosses, then the algae. Beyond the algae were what? In the fragmentary records left fossilized in stone we can find only vague evidence.

How, I wonder, did life begin in the first place? Has life originated only once? What event, what unusual combination of circumstances brought the necessary chemical elements into the proper relationship to produce the thing we call life? So far we do not know the answers. There is one thing that most scientists do agree upon, that all living things are related to each other and thus had a common origin. Man has always attempted to explain his own origins and his past. He would like to know from whence he came and where he is going. This, of course, is the basis of all religions, from those of ancient man to the present. Yet religions and doctrines pass away and we are left with the "great question" unanswered. As a biologist, I have given the matter much thought across the years. I have peered into deep space through my own astronomical telescope and seen the myriads of distant bodies in the heavens, bodies so remote that millions of light-years are required for their light to reach us. They are out there in infinite number and I see no reason to believe that ours is the only heavenly body capable of supporting the miracle we call life. One day, perhaps, we may journey to the stars but, for the present, our way is blocked by time and infinite distance.

It is a common habit for writers of science fiction to people remote planets with strange beasts and even stranger men. The truth is that physical forces and chemical elements are about the same throughout the universe, so why should the inhabitants of remote planets be different at similar stages of evolutionary development? What a surprise it would be to future space travelers to find, after landing upon a far-off world, that they had descended onto a peaceful meadow where cows grazed contentedly upon lush clover and to see, upon a distant hill, the familiar form of a red barn.

Such are my thoughts as I sit beside the stream. However, I am abruptly brought back to the present by a large swallowtail butterfly that has just alighted upon a rhododendron bloom. There is nothing unusual about this small incident; I see hundreds of these attractive insects flying up and down the stream almost every summer day. Today, though, I have time to think seriously about their graceful and marvelous flight coordination, of the way their muscles and sense organs operate to bring about flight and navigation. It is truly amazing how they can maneuver and alight upon any object that attracts them. Often I have watched when one of them was pursued by a bird; I noted the butterfly's evasive tactics, which I am sure required most precise coordination of all its facilities.

Man has come a long way in his conquest of the air, but when compared to the butterfly he is a clumsy bungler. Someday, perhaps, he may equal or even exceed the insect, but for the present his efforts cannot match its wonderful control and maneuverability. The butterfly carries out all its precise aerial tactics by means of several hundred muscles attached to the interior of its hard exoskeleton. These are arranged in complicated ways to bring about the movements of its wings, to quickly bring about adjustments to cope with the vagaries of air currents. In order to carry out these exacting functions, the butterfly must have navigational instruments of great complexity, as well as an amazingly perfect nervous system to conduct information to its muscles. Its sensory instruments consist of eyes, antennae, and tactile hairs, all interconnected by nerves.

As I watch, the swallowtail finally flutters away and sails down the stream and out of view, leaving me to wonder at its incredible flying ability.

After the butterfly has disappeared, my attention vacillates between the waters of the rushing stream and the surrounding forest. A Carolina wren scolds from a nearby dogwood and at last flies away in search of insect food. Eventually my eyes are attracted to a tiny gnat perched upon a nearby leaf. It is less than an eighth of an inch long and has long, slender legs. It walks slowly across the leaf's green surface, its legs moving in precise coordination, perfectly adapted to their function. Having reached the edge of the leaf, the gnat flies upward, hovering in the air as if suspended by an invisible thread. Shortly, it darts away over the stream and disappears from view. It now occurs to me that I have just seen a creature even better adapted to flight than the swallowtail butterfly. I try to visualize what its minute nervous system must be like. How, I wonder, can all the complex sense organs and the interconnecting nerves required for walking and flight be encompassed in such a diminutive body? Here, certainly, is a case of extreme miniaturization. I can more or less understand the complex workings of the human nervous system or that of a cat. As a zoologist, I have studied them in some detail. I can even understand the nervous system of the swallowtail butterfly, because I have dissected one of these insects and observed its details under a microscope. In the case of the gnat, however, I find mystery beyond my understanding. My mind cannot conceive of such amazing reduction in size, along with the complex detail of its parts. How can its leg muscles bring about their precise coordinated movement? These legs are no larger than a hair. Yet, enclosed within them are many muscles and connecting nerves, all operating together to move them in such a manner as to

A rare albino tree squirrel was photographed in the Smoky Mountain forest.

bring about mobility. Even more complex are the muscles and nerves used by the insect for flight. I recall the large banks of navigational instruments present in an airplane. In order to fly, any animal—or airplane—must have a continuous stream of sensory information. The tiny gnat has all this and much more, and I am left to ponder over the marvelous structure of these little insects. Science probes into Nature's mysteries but some of her mysteries are difficult to understand.

The trails of the Smoky Mountains are many. Some follow along the streams, others climb up the steep slopes and meander across level forested areas. Some pass waterfalls of great beauty where mosses and ferns thrive with their feet in the moist soil. Especially in spring there are flowers of great variety along the way, as well as flowering trees rising far overhead. These include silverbells, magnolias, and dogwoods. April is the time when the forests turn white with dogwoods and they are

again white in late May when the mountain laurels open their
delicate blooms. Frequently, the hiker may glimpse the fleeting
form of a deer, half-hidden among the lush vegetation. This is a
place of sylvan beauty where ancient mountains repose in quiet
grandeur, pervaded by an enduring sense of peace.

I often explore these trails and streams, sometimes accompanied by my wife. At especially attractive sites she frequently
sets up her easel and paints. Today, for example, we hiked up
Little River, the place I have called Hidden Valley, and she set
up her equipment beside what is known locally as the Blue
Pool. Only a few of us know this attractive place and to these
chosen few it remains a well-guarded secret.

The Blue Pool is located at a bend in Little River just below
a tumbling cataract. On the opposite side of the pool is a great,
lichen-covered boulder rising more than twenty feet above the
still waters. At certain times of the day the pool takes on a
bluish tint from which it derives its name. It is well hidden by
dense and impenetrable growths of rhododendrons whose
trunks intermingle in such a manner as to make ingress nearly
impossible except at one point where a dim trail, difficult to see,
zigzags down to the pool.

Here, this afternoon, my wife has begun recording the surrounding beauty. Within a few minutes she utters a low excla-
mation and points toward the rapids. There I see a cub bear
jumping from stone to stone as it crosses the stream and disappears among the rhododendrons beyond.

Painting is a slow and detailed process, and thus I have
ample time to explore while she works. Some distance downstream from the Blue Pool I find a number of flowers, among
which are several cancerroots, attractive little flowers about
four inches tall, devoid of leaves and green chlorophyll. I am
always intrigued by these and related plants, since they have
adopted a strange way of life; instead of manufacturing their
own food as do most plants, they attach their roots to those of

Clockwise from top: *Lady's-slipper orchids in the Smokies. The deep purple of pawpaw. Blooms of silverbell trees appear in spring. Squawroot attaches its roots to those of trees. Little brown jugs nestle close to the ground.*

other plants to steal their nutrients. Thus, they are parasitic, a habit common to all members of the strange broomrape family. Other members of this unusual family are found at various locations in the mountains. One is squawroot, looking a little like a pale white pine cone growing out of the earth. It is also known as "bear-corn" and obtains its nourishment from the roots of oaks and other trees. Still another broomrape are the beechdrops, having pale yellowish or purplish flowers. As their name implies, they are parasitic on the roots of beech trees.

Near the Blue Pool I also discover a number of small oil nut trees, a common inhabitant of Appalachian forests. At this season they bear clusters of small greenish flowers, but by autumn they will have oil-filled nuts about an inch in diameter. The oil within these nuts is said to be poisonous. These small trees, or shrubs, have green leaves like any other tree, but supplement their nourishment by attaching their roots to those of rhododendrons and other plants. Apparently, the parasitic habit "runs in families." The oil nut is a member of the sandalwood family, whose members occur in many tropical lands. One kind, the scented sandalwood tree, is common in Hawaii where I have seen it growing. Its wood is used for making furniture and as a source of perfume. Distantly related to the sandalwoods are the parasitic mistletoes, found in many parts of the world, as well as here in the Smokies.

Seemingly, the parasitic habit is especially prevalent in areas where there is relentless competition among plants for space and nourishment. This, certainly, is true of the Smoky Mountains where plants thrive abundantly and compete for every square inch of earth and sun.

By this time the sun has descended below the crest of the mountains, leaving the Blue Pool in gloom. Annie Laurie can no longer paint, since the great pyramid rock beyond the pool is now in deep shadow. We pack up and leave, hurrying away through the darkening forest.

Probably our greatest single source of enjoyment at our mountain retreat is the trail beyond Jakes Creek. The trail follows along the creek, descending from the remote reaches of the distant mountains, now inhabited only by wild creatures. There dwell bears, bobcats, raccoons, mink, skunks, foxes, tree squirrels, and rabbits. Once there were panthers and wolves, but they are gone, destroyed by the settlers who once lived here. Now and then there are reports of panthers, but none of these can be confirmed. The last authentic sighting of a panther occurred near Fighting Creek Gap about 1925. This is only a couple of miles from Elkmont.

Up and down the Jakes Creek trail, at one time or another, pass almost all the mountain animals. A few, less elusive than others, use the trail during the daylight hours. One afternoon a mother mink and four young hurried down the trail. She led the way, her young following so closely behind as to remind us of an undulating snake.

It is at night, however, that most of the mountain creatures pass up and down the trail, showing themselves in our floodlights. It is a situation remindful of the tree-hotels near water holes in South Africa where tourists may watch, in comfort and safety, the antics of elephants and other beasts.

Our first summer on Jakes Creek turned out to be the "summer of the skunks." Skunks were seen everywhere, even during the daytime. They established dens under many of our neighbors' cottages and reared their young. On many nights we could count half a dozen at once, cavorting under our floodlights where we had placed food. The strange thing was that we got all the "credit" for the tremendous influx of skunks, which, I suppose, was understandable since it was our first summer there and it was known that we regularly put out food to attract wild animals. The truth, of course, is that skunk populations tend to be cyclic, frequently becoming very abundant in areas where there are usually very few. We denied

The rear windows of our summer cottage in the Smoky Mountains overlook Jakes Creek. Floodlights illuminate the stream and the trail just beyond at night.

responsibility for the sudden explosion of the local skunk population. However, whether they were skunk lovers or not, our neighbors regularly congregated at our cottage to watch the "Hutchins' skunks."

These skunks were mostly very attractive, their coloration varying from solid black to solid white or combinations thereof. One night a gray fox came down the trail while several skunks were feeding. The fox sat down and watched, never venturing near them. Only after the skunks had finished feeding and gone did the fox have enough courage to approach the food. It was obvious that the fox had great respect for its malodorous neighbors.

I am happy to report that the next summer the skunk population of the mountains had dwindled down to normal and that our neighbors no longer regarded us with suspicion. As a matter of fact, they admitted that they missed watching the skunks in their nocturnal forays under our floodlights.

One night, near midnight, I was idly watching the trail when a bobcat walked slowly by. Usually we kept food at the point on the trail most easily seen from our picture windows but, on this night, there was no food and so the cat passed on down the trail and out of sight.

Foxes were and are our most dependable visitors, usually appearing at about the same hour, generally at about ten o'clock. We have noticed that some of them are very nervous, while others are completely at ease. Air movement is usually downstream at night and, as a result, the foxes always watch down the creek. Their sensitive noses, I suppose, tell them what is upstream and so they watch for danger from below, well aware of any threat lurking above.

One summer night we saw a large bear and her cub come ambling down the trail. She was leading the way, with the cub close behind. Our rear windows are about fifteen feet above the creek and so my wife felt secure both by our height and the width of the stream separating the bears from us. However, the mother bear finally decided to cross over to our side, an act requiring only a couple of short jumps. This put an entirely

Skunks often pass down the trail beyond the stream. They feed upon food placed there.

Raccoons frequently appear under the floodlights. Foxes are also regular visitors.

Bears are common and, usually, welcome visitors. Sometimes they come down the trail beyond Jakes Creek.

different aspect on things and my wife became much concerned. Eventually, though, the bears went on down Jakes Creek and out of sight in the darkness.

The truth is that bears are quite unpredictable and a person never knows how they will react. On several occasions I have blundered onto them in the dark, but never into actual contact. However, one dark night a neighbor walked into a bear in front of our cottage and it was a tossup as to which one was frightened the most. In any case, the bear uttered a couple of loud woofs and took off up the mountainside. Certainly a bear should always be treated with great respect.

Of our daytime visitors, the crows are the most vociferous. They gather each morning to eat the scraps we toss out along the stream. They are greedy creatures, always attempting to carry off every scrap in sight, even though their beaks already hold all a crow can handle. Our most amusing incident with these birds occurred one day when we had thrown out a pan of spaghetti. This food was definitely beyond the crows' experi-

A deer mouse and her young were found in a rotten log.

Chipmunks outwitted me, stealing food from my bird feeder. They hibernate in winter.

ence and gave them much difficulty. The slick strings usually slipped out of their beaks. When this happened the crow would hop back and study the strange food, then try again. The most amusing part of the performance was when a crow attempted to add a second helping of spaghetti to that already in its beak. Naturally, the first piece fell out, making it necessary for the frustrated crow to start all over again.

Since the above incident occurred we have several times prepared spaghetti crow-bait to amuse friends. I am sure that we have by now the most frustrated and, perhaps, neurotic crows in the Smoky Mountains. Crows, however, are intelligent and wary, a fact, I suppose, that accounts for there being so many of them. Beside the stream we have several aluminum chairs and if any food falls beneath one of them, the crows hop around it in frustration, looking longingly at it but never venturing to retrieve the food. These chairs are something beyond their comprehension and they are afraid to approach one.

Regarding frustration, I have, myself, become afflicted by a severe case, due to chipmunks. I enjoy having these alert little animals around, but I have long since decided that they are smarter than I am. In an effort to attract birds, I attached a bird feeder to the trunk of a large hemlock near the creek. The bird feeder was located about ten feet from the ground and it never occurred to me that chipmunks would rob it. The chipmunks I knew in the Rockies rarely left the ground and I assumed that the Smoky Mountain species had similar habits. Much to my surprise, these Smoky Mountain chipmunks could easily climb more than twenty feet up a tree. This, I suppose, was to be expected in a region of dense forests.

To foil the chipmunks I enclosed the hemlock trunk with a wrapping of plastic, hoping that the chipmunks could not climb over it. They couldn't. However, the ingenious little creatures soon discovered a way to "worm" up under the plastic. Then, in a further effort to outwit them, I hoisted the bird feeder higher, suspending it from a limb so that it was about two feet away from the trunk. This gave the chipmunks no trouble at all; they simply climbed up the trunk and jumped across to the bird feeder. So, in the end, I gave up, deciding to feed chipmunks instead of song birds. I am at least smart enough to know when I am confronted by intelligence and capabilities greater than my own. I have definitely been outwitted.

Here in the Great Smoky Mountains we dwell against an always-changing background of sylvan beauty in a glen secluded and still. It is a place to remember and to plan for future projects. It is a place, I like to think, where all birds sing, where even the raucous calls of the crows at dawn are pleasing to the ear. The songs of the mountain birds seem endowed with a special accent, voicing their happiness and joy of living.

Often, at dusk, when the birds are stilled and I have only the sounds of the mountain stream for company, I gaze across the tumbling water, watching for whatever four-footed inhabitants may pass down the trail beyond. It occurs to me that I have always been following trails of one sort or another. Some have led to small adventures, others have revealed unsuspected secrets. The trails I have followed are of many kinds, but all trails lead to somewhere. But it is not the trails themselves that are of interest; it is where they go or what is seen along the way. Those to remote and little-known places have always intrigued me.

My own trails have led over mountains, across deserts, or through jungles and tropical swamplands. They have followed along the beaches of South Pacific islands and penetrated the tangled depths of mangrove swamps. Some of these trails were man-made, others resulted from the hurrying feet of wild beasts in their restless wanderings. Always there has been the thrill of discovery, of seeing what lay beyond the next bend.

INDEX

Page numbers in **boldface** *are those on which illustrations appear.*

217

ABOUT THE AUTHOR

ENTOMOLOGIST ROSS E. HUTCHINS is also an expert nature photographer, and this combination of interests has resulted in more than thirty years of studying, photographing, and writing about insects, plants, animals, and birds. Born in Montana, he grew up on a cattle ranch near Yellowstone National Park. At Montana State College he majored in biological sciences and later he received his PhD. in zoology and entomology from Iowa State College. During World War II he served as an Epidemic Disease Control Officer, with the rank of Lieutenant Commander.

Dr. Hutchins' articles and pictures of natural history subjects have appeared in encyclopedias, books, and magazines, including European publications. His most recent adult book was *Hidden Valley of the Smokies*, a naturalist's adventures in the Great Smoky Mountains. His many juvenile titles include *Insects and Their Young, Grasshoppers and Their Kin, The Amazing Seeds, The Bug Clan, This Is a Tree*. All are noted for their remarkable close-up photographs by the author.

Ross Hutchins was for many years Director of the State Plant Board of Mississippi and is Professor Emeritus of Entomology at Mississippi State University. He lives in Mississippi and the Great Smoky Mountains, devoting his time to travel, writing, and photographing plant and animal life. He is listed in *Who's Who* and *American Men of Science*.